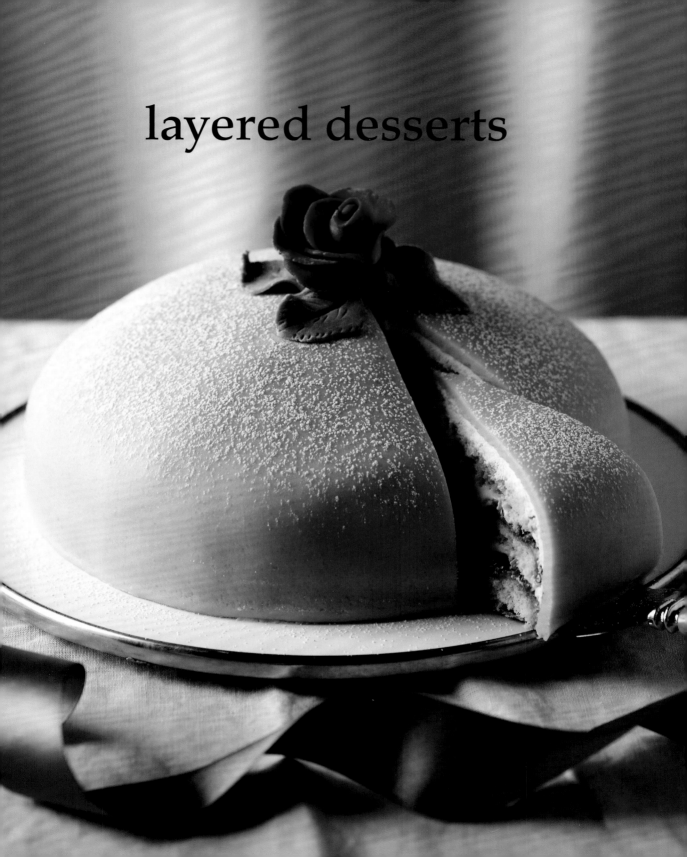

layered desserts

layered desserts

Hannah Miles

photography by Steve Painter

RYLAND PETERS & SMALL
LONDON • NEW YORK

*For my fabulous friend
Maren, with love and
friendship x*

**Design, photography and prop
styling** Steve Painter
Editors Kate Eddison, Alice
Sambrook and Gillian Haslam
Production Gordana Simakovic
Art Director Leslie Harrington
Editorial Director Julia Charles
Publisher Cindy Richards

Food Stylist Lucy McKelvie
Food Stylist's assistant Cherry
Ackerman
Indexer Vanessa Bird

First published in 2016 by
Ryland Peters & Small
20–21 Jockey's Fields
London WC1R 4BW
and
341 East 116th Street
New York NY 10029

www.rylandpeters.com

Text © Hannah Miles 2016

Design and photographs © Ryland
Peters & Small 2016

ISBN: 978-1-84975-763-8

10 9 8 7 6 5 4 3 2 1

Printed and bound in China.

A CIP record for this book is
available from the British Library.
US Library of Congress CIP data
has been applied for.

Notes
• Both British (metric) and American
(imperial plus US cups) are included
in these recipes; however, it is
important to work with one set of
measurements and not alternate
between the two within a recipe.
• All spoon measurements are level
unless otherwise specified.
• All eggs are medium (UK) or large
(US), unless specified as large, in
which case US extra large should be
used. Uncooked or partially cooked
eggs should not be served to the very
old, frail, young children, pregnant
women or those with compromised
immune systems.
• There are certain healthy risk
associated with whipped cream so
always practice food safety by using
fresh cream before its expiry date
and covering and storing prepared
desserts in the refrigerator until
ready to serve.
• When a recipe calls for the grated
zest of citrus fruit, buy unwaxed fruit
and wash well before using. If you
can only find treated fruit, scrub well
in warm soapy water before using.

contents

classic layers

In this chapter you will find layers inspired by much-loved traditional desserts. The delicious Cookies and Cream Delight and rich Black Forest Layer Cake are sure to please. Or try classic Millefeuilles: crisp pastry layers sandwiched together with vanilla crème pâtissière and fresh raspberries, or a dainty and perfectly formed Stripy Passion Fruit and Chocolate Panna Cotta. This chapter also contains a magnificent Spanische Windtorte – a meringue casket decorated with pretty sugar flowers. My version is filled with chocolate cake, cherry compote and whipped cream, but you could choose any filling you like.

Pink meringue layer berry cake

This cake is perfect for a summer's day, with layers of almond sponge and delicate pink meringue all sandwiched together with cream and fresh berries. The cake is topped with pretty meringue peaks which make a spectacular decoration. I took it to my archery club and it was devoured within minutes.

FOR THE ALMOND SPONGE:

225 g/2 sticks butter, softened

225 g/generous 1 cup caster/granulated sugar

4 UK large/US extra-large eggs

115 g/generous 1 cup ground almonds

115 g/³/4 cup plus 2 tablespoons self-raising/self-rising flour, sifted

1 teaspoon baking powder

FOR THE MERINGUE:

3 UK large/US extra-large egg whites

180 g/scant 1 cup caster/granulated sugar

pink food colouring gel or paste

TO ASSEMBLE:

300 ml/1¹/4 cups double/heavy cream

250 g/9 oz. strawberries, hulled and sliced

3 tablespoons strawberry jam/jelly

2 x 20-cm/8-inch round cake pans, greased and lined

large baking sheet, lined with baking parchment

piping/pastry bag fitted with large round nozzle/tip

SERVES 8–10

Preheat the oven to 180°C (350°F) Gas 4.

In a mixing bowl, whisk together the butter and sugar until light and creamy. Whisk in the eggs one at a time and then fold in the ground almonds, self-raising/self-rising flour and baking powder. Divide the mixture between the prepared cake pans and bake in the preheated oven for 20–25 minutes until the cakes are firm and spring back to your touch.

Remove the cakes from the oven, turn out from the cake pans and leave to cool completely. Remove the lining paper and place the two cakes slightly apart on the lined baking sheet.

Reduce the oven temperature to 130°C (250°F) Gas ¹/2.

For the meringue, in a clean bowl, whisk the egg whites to stiff peaks, then add the caster/granulated sugar, a spoonful at a time together with a little pink food colouring gel, whisking all the time, so that the meringue turns a pretty pink colour. The meringue should be stiff and hold a peak when you lift the beaters or whisk.

Spoon the meringue into the piping/pastry bag. Pipe a circle of meringue over the top of one cake in a flat layer. Pipe the remaining meringue in peaks on the other cake, lifting the nozzle/tip up high as you pipe each ball of meringue to make high peaks. Transfer the baking sheet to the oven and bake for 1–1¹/4 hours until the meringue is crisp. Remove from the oven and leave to cool.

When you are ready to serve, whip the cream to stiff peaks. Place the cake with the flat layer of meringue on a serving plate and spoon over the whipped cream. Top with the strawberries and the jam/jelly and then carefully place the peak-topped meringue cake on top. Serve straight away. As the cake contains fresh cream, any uneaten cake should be stored in the refrigerator and is best eaten within 2 days.

Black Forest layer cake

This cake has a rich chocolate brownie later, whipped cream and cherry compote topped with a light cherry sponge. Wrapped in silky chocolate ganache – it is the perfect retro dessert!

FOR THE CHERRY SPONGE:

115 g/generous ½ cup caster/granulated sugar

115 g/1 stick butter, softened

2 UK large/US extra-large eggs

115 g/¾ cup plus 2 tablespoons self-raising/self-rising flour, sifted

1 teaspoon pure vanilla extract

1 tablespoon low-fat natural/plain yogurt

260 g/9 oz. canned black cherries in syrup, drained weight

FOR THE BROWNIE LAYER:

200 g/7 oz. plain/semisweet chocolate, broken into pieces

125 g/9 tablespoons butter

2 UK large/US extra-large eggs

200 g/1 cup caster/granulated sugar

100 g/¾ cup plain/all-purpose flour, sifted

1 teaspoon pure vanilla extract

FOR THE GANACHE:

100 g/3½ oz. plain/semisweet chocolate

1 tablespoon liquid glucose

1 heaped tablespoon butter

100 ml/⅓ cup double/heavy cream

2 tablespoons icing/confectioners' sugar, sifted

TO ASSEMBLE:

150 ml/⅔ cup double/heavy cream

3 tablespoons cherry compote

10 whole cherries

50 g/2 oz. white chocolate

2 x 20-cm/8-inch square cake pan, greased and lined

piping/pastry bag

SERVES 10

Preheat the oven to 180°C (350°F) Gas 4.

For the cherry sponge, whisk together the caster/granulated sugar and butter until light and creamy. Beat in the eggs, one at a time, whisking after each egg is added. Sift in the flour and add the vanilla and fold in gently with the yogurt. Spoon into one of the prepared cake pans and cover with a layer of the drained cherries, distributing them evenly. Bake for 40–45 minutes, until a sharp knife inserted into the centre comes out clean.

For the brownie layer, melt the chocolate and butter in a saucepan resting over a pan of simmering water and leave to cool. In a separate bowl, whisk together the eggs and caster/granulated sugar until very thick and creamy. Gently fold in the melted chocolate mixture, plain/all-purpose flour and vanilla. Spoon into the second cake pan. Bake in the preheated oven for 25–30 minutes until a crust has formed on top and the cake still feels soft underneath.

You can bake both cakes at the same time as the pans should fit side by side in the oven, removing the brownie cake after the shorter cooking time. Leave the brownie to cool in the pan and turn the cake out onto a wire rack. Leave both cakes to cool.

For the ganache, break the chocolate into pieces and place in a heatproof bowl with the liquid glucose, butter and cream and set over a pan of simmering water. Stir until melted and you have a thick glossy sauce. Sift in the icing/confectioners' sugar, beat into the ganache for a few seconds, just until the icing sugar has dissolved. Leave to cool slightly.

To assemble, whip the double/heavy cream to stiff peaks. Remove the brownie from the pan and peel away the lining paper. Place on a cooling rack with a piece of foil underneath to catch any ganache drips. Top with the whipped cream and then spoon over the cherry compote. Top with the cherry sponge and then spread the ganache over the top and sides of the cake using a round-bladed knife or spatula.

Break the white chocolate into pieces and place in a heatproof bowl resting over a pan of simmering water and heat until melted. Spoon into a piping/pastry bag and pipe thin rectangles of white chocolate over the top of the cake. Alternatively, drizzle thin lines with a fork. Place the whole cherries on top and carefully transfer the cake to a serving plate. Chill in the refrigerator until you are ready to serve. The cake will store for up to 2 days in the refrigerator.

Salted caramel apple Napoleons

These delicious pastry slices are filled with a boozy apple cream and slices of toffee-coated apple. They make a perfect treat for afternoon tea or can be dressed up as a more elegant dessert, served with pouring cream and extra toffee sauce.

375 g/13 oz. all-butter puff pastry

1 UK large/US extra-large egg, beaten

3 eating apples

15 g/1 tablespoon butter

2 tablespoons soft dark brown sugar

45 ml/3 tablespoons apple schnapps (such as Apfelkorn) or apple juice

pinch of salt

plain/all-purpose flour, for dusting

caster/granulated sugar, for sprinkling

icing/confectioners' sugar, for dusting

FOR THE CREAM:

200 ml/generous 3/4 cup double/heavy cream

45 ml/3 tablespoons apple schnapps (such as Apfelkorn)

7-cm/3-inch triangle cutter

large baking sheets, lined with silicon mats or baking parchment

MAKES 6

Preheat the oven to 200°C (400°F) Gas 6.

On a flour-dusted surface, roll out the pastry very thinly into a large rectangle using a rolling pin. Cut out 18 triangles of pastry using the cutter (or a sharp knife) and place a small distance apart on the lined baking sheet. Brush the top of the pastry triangles with the beaten egg and sprinkle with a little caster/granulated sugar. Cover with a second sheet of baking parchment and place a large baking sheet on top to weigh the pastry down. This will ensure that you get very thin layers of crisp pastry that hold their shape.

Bake in the preheated oven for 20–30 minutes until the pastry is crisp and golden brown. Lift off the second baking sheet and leave the pastry triangles on the sheet to cool.

Core the apples and cut into thin slices. You can leave the skin on the apples or remove it depending on your preference. I like to leave it on and use red apples as this gives a pretty colour contrast. Place the apple slices in a large frying pan/skillet with the butter and one tablespoon of the soft dark brown sugar and fry until the apples start to soften. Add the apple schnapps to the pan with the second tablespoon of sugar and a good pinch of salt, and cook over the heat until the apples start to caramelize. Remove from the heat and leave to cool.

When you are ready to serve, place the cream and apple schnapps in a mixing bowl and whisk to soft peaks.

To assemble the pastries, place a spoonful of the whipped cream on top of six of the triangles and top with some of the apple slices. Cover each with a second pastry triangle and again top with cream and apples. Place the remaining triangles on top and dust with icing/confectioners' sugar. Serve straight away or store in the refrigerator as the pastries contain fresh cream. The pastries are best eaten on the day they are assembled, although you can cook the pastry the day before if you wish.

Cookies and cream delight

This indulgent dessert combines the favourite combination of cookies and cream – it is what I bring out as my party treat as it always gets lots of 'oohs' and 'ahhs' and tastes absolutely delicious. You can substitute other cookies for the Oreos if you have another favourite, such as a selection of pink wafers or party rings for a perfectly kitsch look.

FOR THE CHOCOLATE SAUCE:

100 g/3½ oz. plain/semisweet chocolate

250 ml/1 cup double/heavy cream

60 g/½ stick butter

1 tablespoon liquid glucose

FOR THE COOKIE CREAM:

600 ml/2½ cups double/heavy cream

200 g/7 oz. cream cheese

2 tablespoons icing/confectioners' sugar, sifted

½ teaspoon vanilla bean powder or 1 teaspoon pure vanilla extract

150 g/5½ oz. Oreo cookies

TO ASSEMBLE:

1 large chocolate Swiss roll/jelly roll (approx. 340 g/¾ lb.)

unsweetened cocoa powder, for dusting

mini Oreo cookies, for decoration

large glass bowl

SERVES 10

For the chocolate sauce, break the chocolate into pieces and place in a saucepan with the cream, butter and liquid glucose, and simmer over a gentle heat until the butter and chocolate have melted and you have a smooth glossy sauce. Set aside to cool.

For the cookie cream, in a mixing bowl whisk together the double/heavy cream and cream cheese until smooth and thick. Whisk in the icing/confectioners' sugar and vanilla. Reserve six of the standard-sized Oreo cookies and crush the remainder into small pieces and fold into the cream.

Cut the chocolate Swiss roll/jelly roll into thin slices and place half of them over the base of the dish. Crush three of the remaining cookies and sprinkle over the Swiss roll/jelly roll slices. Pour over half of the chocolate sauce. Spoon over half of the cream and spread out into an even layer. Cover with further slices of Swiss roll/jelly roll and repeat the steps above ending with a top layer of the cookie cream. Dust with a generous layer of cocoa powder and decorate with mini Oreos. Chill in the refrigerator for at least 3 hours or overnight before serving. This trifle will keep for up to 3 days covered in the refrigerator.

Spanische windtorte

Where to begin? This can only be described as an 'epic' dessert given the steps involved and the end result! It was made popular on the well-known UK television baking competition, The Great British Bake Off and I can safely say that if you want to bring a dessert to the table that will make your guests say 'wow' then this is the one to make. Despite its title, the dessert is actually of Austrian origin rather than Spanish. It is said to have become popular in the Baroque period with the Spanish influence coming from the nobility's love of all things related to Spain.

In essence this delectable dessert is a casket made from meringue, decorated with piped meringue and sugar flowers, topped with a pretty lid and filled with cream and fruits of your choice. The possibilities are endless for decorations and fillings and you can really go to town and create the perfect meringue fantasy cake. It takes time – I am not going to lie to you – but most of the time is spent baking the meringue shells, so the actual work involved inbetween cooking is fairly reasonable. The meringue shell can be made the day before (or over several days) and just filled on the day you want to serve it.

The recipe uses two types of meringue, which gives different textures – a hard French meringue which is used to make the main meringue rings and lid, and then a softer Swiss meringue for the decoration piping. The Swiss meringue is made using a hot sugar syrup which cooks the meringue and means that it requires less time baking.

The casket is created by piping two discs of meringue and then about four hoops of meringue which are cooked until crisp. Once they have cooled, you can stack the rings on top of one of the discs with more soft meringue to make the casket. If you are feeling extra creative, you could add a few drops of food colouring to some of the meringue so that when the cake is cut you have a pretty striped effect within the meringue.

Have fun with the meringue decoration. I love to try out all different types of piping nozzles/tips as they all create such different patterns. It is worth spending a few minutes experimenting before you start piping. Having a rotating table or lazy susan really helps when you are piping to ensure that your decorations are in even rings around the cake.

The windtorte is traditionally topped with sugar violets, which you can make yourself from sugar paste coloured with a little purple food colouring, but they are also available to buy from cake decorating shops and larger supermarkets/stores. If you cannot find sugar violets, then any colour or variety of sugar flowers will look equally pretty.

When it comes to filling the casket, again the possibilities are endless. This indulgent recipe uses thin layers of chocolate cake, cherry compote and fresh whipped cream but you could fill with anything you choose – strawberry mousse, raspberries and fresh cream or simply cream layered with fresh fruits. If you wished, you could make mini individual windtorte by scaling down the size of the meringue rings.

This is not a cake for every day, but it is definitely one that will make you proud to have achieved such an impressive bake in your own kitchen, so I do urge you to try it!

FOR THE FIRST MERINGUE:

4 UK large/US extra-large egg whites

225 g/generous 1 cup caster/granulated sugar

FOR THE SECOND MERINGUE:

2 UK large/US extra-large egg whites

115 g/generous 1/2 cup caster/granulated sugar

FOR THE THIRD MERINGUE:

4 UK large/US extra-large egg whites

250 g/1 1/4 cups caster/granulated sugar

FOR THE CAKE:

115 g/generous 1/2 cup caster/granulated sugar

115 g/1 stick butter, softened

2 UK large/US extra-large eggs

115 g/3/4 cup plus 2 tablespoons self-raising/self-rising flour, sifted

30 g/1/3 cup unsweetened cocoa powder, sifted

2 tablespoons natural/plain yogurt

FOR THE FILLING:

600 ml/2 1/2 cups heavy/double cream

1 tablespoon icing/confectioners' sugar, sifted

1/2 teaspoon vanilla bean powder or 1 teaspoon pure vanilla extract

400 g/14 oz. cherry compote

TO DECORATE:

sugar flowers, traditionally sugar violets or fondant violets

3 baking sheets, lined with silicon mats or baking parchment

2 piping/pastry bags fitted with round nozzle/tip and star nozzle/tip

20-cm/8-inch round cake pan, greased and lined

SERVES 12

Preheat the oven to 130°C (250°F) Gas 1/2.

For the first meringue, whisk the egg whites to very stiff peaks and then whisk in the caster/granulated sugar, a spoonful at a time, until you have a glossy meringue. Spoon the meringue into the piping/pastry bag fitted with the large round nozzle/tip.

With the first meringue you need to pipe two whole discs of meringue and four rings of meringue all of the same size. If you are using baking parchment, draw round an 18-cm/7-inch plate on the underside of the paper and use this as a template for your piping.

I use silicon mats as I find the meringues are easier to remove from these. Therefore, rather than drawing a template, I pipe around an 18-cm/7-inch plate, piping just a little away from the edge of the plate. Once you have piped the ring of the meringue, carefully remove the plate. I do this by sliding a knife underneath and, while pressing down firmly on the top of the plate, use the knife to lever the plate up. Don't worry if the plate touches the meringue as it will all be covered with a further layer of meringue in the next baking stage.

On the four meringue rings, pipe a second layer of meringue on top of the rings to make them higher. With the two remaining meringues, fill the circle to make discs by piping a spiral of meringue in each, making sure that there are no gaps. I use three large baking sheets and pipe two meringues onto each.

Bake the meringues in the oven for about 1-1 1/2 hours until the meringue rings and discs are crisp. If you are baking the sheets of meringue in the oven at the same time, the lower sheets will take longer to cook than the top sheets, depending on the heat in your oven. Leave the meringues to cool completely. Keep the oven on for the next batch.

For the second meringue, whisk the egg whites to stiff peaks and then, as before, whisk in the caster/granulated sugar, a spoonful at a time, until the meringue is smooth and glossy.

Leave one of the flat discs of meringue aside, as you will not need this until the next stage, and place the other whole disc of meringue into the centre of one of the baking sheets. Taking great care, one by one lift the meringue rings and place on top of the meringue disc, fixing in place with a little of the second meringue mixture. You want to stack the rings so that they make a casket with the disc on the base as the bottom of the casket. Using the remaining second meringue and a spatula, gently spread a thin layer of meringue over the outside and inside of the sides of the casket so that the individual rings from the first baking are all covered and your casket has smooth sides. If any of the meringue rings break when you lift them, do not worry and simply stick them in place on top of one of the other rings with a little of the second meringue.

Bake in the oven for a further hour or so until the meringue casket is crisp. Remove from the oven and leave to cool. Leave the oven on.

The third meringue is a Swiss meringue and is cooked over the heat. Place a large mixing bowl over a pan of simmering water and add the egg whites and sugar together. Whisk all the time until you have a thick meringue mixture. This will take about 5 minutes using an electric whisk (you can use a hand whisk which will take longer and will make your arm hurt!). Remove from the heat and continue to whisk until the meringue cools. Spoon the meringue into the piping/pastry bag fitted with a star nozzle/tip and pipe rings of stars around the casket and on the reserved second disc, which will act as the lid for the torte. You can be as creative as you want with the meringue decoration and use different shaped nozzles/tips if your piping/pastry bag has an interchangeable fixing. Bake the casket and lid in the oven for about 30 minutes until the Swiss meringue is firm. Leave to cool. Increase the oven temperature to 180°C (350°F) Gas 4.

For the cake, whisk together the caster/granulated sugar and butter until light and creamy. Add the eggs, one at a time, whisking after each egg is added. Gently fold in the sifted flour, cocoa powder and yogurt. Spoon the cake mixture into the prepared cake pan and bake for 20–25 minutes until the cake is firm and springs back to your touch and a knife comes out clean when inserted into the centre. Leave to cool.

Using a sharp knife, trim the cake so that it is just smaller than the size of the cavity of your casket. Cut the cake in half horizontally so that you have two discs of cake.

For the filling, in a mixing bowl, whisk the double/heavy cream, icing/confectioners' sugar and vanilla to stiff peaks.

Now it is time to fill your Windtorte! Lift the Windtorte very carefully to a serving plate or cake stand. Reserve a few spoonfuls of the cream for sticking on the flowers later. Spoon one-third of the cream into the cavity and top with one-third of the cherry compote. Place one of the cakes on top and then cover with another one-third of the cream and another one-third of the cherries. Place the second cake on top and cover with the remaining cream and cherries. Cover the Windtorte with the meringue lid. Decorate with the sugar flowers, fixing them in place with a little of the reserved cream.

Serve straight away, and be prepared for a fleeting rush of sadness when you cut the cake, destroying all your hard work in a matter of seconds! Any uneaten meringue should be stored in the refrigerator for 2 days.

Classic trifle with summer berries

Trifle is one of the most traditional of British desserts. There is quite a debate about whether a traditional trifle should include jelly/Jello or not – my view is not but that is only because I don't really like jelly/Jello. If you want you can make up a packet of strawberry jelly following the packet instructions and add it over the fruit layer if you wish.

FOR THE CREME PATISSIERE:

2 UK large/US extra-large eggs, plus 2 yolks

2 heaped tablespoons cornflour/cornstarch

$1/2$ teaspoon vanilla bean powder or 1 teaspoon pure vanilla extract

120 g/generous $1/2$ cup caster/granulated sugar

300 ml/$1 1/4$ cups double/heavy cream

200 ml/generous $3/4$ cup milk

FOR THE COMPOTE:

300 g/$10 1/2$ oz. raspberries

300 g/$10 1/2$ oz. blueberries

100 g/ $1/2$ cup caster/granulated sugar

TO ASSEMBLE:

2 small raspberry Swiss rolls/jelly rolls or 1 large raspberry Swiss roll/jelly roll (weighing approx. 400 g/14 oz.)

160 ml/scant $3/4$ cup sherry

600 ml/$2 1/2$ cups double/heavy cream

large trifle dish

SERVES 8

Begin by preparing the crème pâtissière as it needs to cool before you assemble the trifle. Whisk together the eggs, egg yolks, cornflour/cornstarch, vanilla and caster/granulated sugar. Heat the cream and milk together in a saucepan and bring to the boil then pour over the egg mixture, whisking all the time. If you do not have a stand mixer, get someone to help pour the milk mixture while you whisk. Return the mixture to the saucepan and simmer over a gentle heat, whisking all the time until the custard thickens, then immediately pour into a bowl. If you leave it in the pan it will continue to cook and may scramble. If your mixture does start to scramble, quickly pour it into a fine-mesh sieve/strainer and whisk hard in the sieve/strainer so that it passes into a bowl below – the scrambled parts will recombine with the custard. Leave to cool.

Next prepare the compote. Heat half of the raspberries and half of the blueberries in a saucepan with the caster/granulated sugar and 2 tablespoons of water and simmer for about 5 minutes until the fruit is soft and the juice is syrupy. Leave to cool.

To assemble, cut the Swiss roll/jelly roll into thick slices and place over the base and lower sides of the dish. Drizzle over the sherry and then spoon over the fruit compote. Top with the remaining fresh berries and then pour over the cooled custard.

Whip the cream to soft peaks in a bowl and spoon over the top of the trifle. Chill in the refrigerator for about 3 hours. To serve, you can top with more berries if you wish. The trifle will keep for up to 3 days in the refrigerator.

Millefeuilles

Millefeuilles means 'a thousand leaves', representing the many pastry layers in this delicious slice. Baking the pastry with a baking sheet on top will ensure the slices keep their shape.

FOR THE PASTRY:

500 g/1 lb. 2 oz. all-butter puff pastry

plain/all-purpose flour, for dusting

milk, to glaze

caster/granulated sugar, for sprinkling

FOR THE CREME PATISSIERE:

125 ml/1/2 cup milk

125 ml/1/2 cup double/heavy cream

1 UK large/US extra-large egg, plus 2 yolks

100 g/1/2 cup caster/granulated sugar

2 tablespoons cornflour/cornstarch

TO ASSEMBLE:

300 ml/11/4 cups double/heavy cream

1/2 teaspoon vanilla bean powder or 1 teaspoon pure vanilla extract

1 tablespoon icing/confectioners' sugar, sifted, plus extra for dusting

300 g/101/2 oz. raspberries

6 tablespoons raspberry jam/jelly

2 baking sheets, 1 lined with a silicon mat or baking parchment

piping/pastry bag fitted with large star nozzle/tip

MAKES 6

Begin by making the crème pâtissière as it needs to chill in the refrigerator before being used. In a saucepan bring the milk and cream to the boil. Meanwhile, in a mixing bowl whisk together the egg, egg yolks, sugar and cornflour/cornstarch until thick and creamy. Pour over the boiling cream mixture and whisk for a few minutes. Return the custard to the pan and heat over a gentle heat, whisking all the time until the custard starts to thicken. Watch it carefully as it can easily turn into a scrambled egg-like mixture. Pass the custard through a fine-mesh sieve/strainer, scraping through with a spatula to get rid of any lumps. Leave to cool and then chill in the refrigerator. It is important that you cool the custard completely so that it is thick and not too runny.

Preheat the oven to 200°C (400°F) Gas 6.

Roll the pastry out thinly into a large rectangle, about 3 mm/1/8 inch thick. Cut the pastry into three long equal rectangles using a sharp knife, trimming the sides and ends to make them even. Place the pastry strips on the lined baking sheet. Brush the tops with a little milk and sprinkle lightly with caster/granulated sugar. Cover the pastry with another sheet of baking parchment and place a second baking sheet on top.

Bake in the preheated oven for 30–35 minutes until the pastry is crisp and golden brown. Check towards the end of cooking to ensure that the pastry does not burn. Once cooked, slide the pastry slices onto a cooling rack and leave to cool completely.

When you are ready to assemble, cut each pastry slice into six even slices, giving you a total of 18 pastry rectangles. Place six slices of pastry on a serving plate. Place the double/heavy cream, vanilla and icing/confectioners' sugar in a mixing bowl and whisk to stiff peaks. Spoon the thick cream into the piping/pastry bag and pipe small stars of cream around the edge of the six pastry slices, leaving a gap between each. Place a raspberry into each of the gaps. There should be a small cavity in the middle of the pastry and you should spoon or pipe a little of the cooled crème pâtissière into this. Place a small spoon of raspberry jam/jelly on top of the custard.

Place a second slice of pastry on top of each and then repeat the steps above, ending with a final pastry slice on top. Dust with icing/confectioners' sugar and chill in the refrigerator until ready to serve. They are best eaten on the day they are assembled (although you can prepare the pastry the day before), but will keep for 2 days stored in the refrigerator.

Pistachio and chocolate marquise

This is a delicate terrine, filled with chocolate ganache, layered and encased in a pistachio sponge and covered with cream and pretty green pistachios. Although the ganache is rich, the sponge is very light, so they make a perfect pairing.

FOR THE SPONGE:

4 UK large/US extra-large eggs

115 g/generous 1/2 cup caster/
granulated sugar

115 g/3/4 cup plus 2 tablespoons
self-raising/self-rising flour, sifted

1 teaspoon baking powder

100 g/31/2 oz. pistachios, finely
chopped

FOR THE MARQUISE:

300 g/101/2 oz. plain/semisweet
chocolate

150 g/11/4 sticks butter, softened

160 g/generous 3/4 cup caster/
granulated sugar

2 tablespoons cocoa powder,
sifted

4 UK large/US extra-large egg
yolks

150 ml/2/3 cup double/heavy
cream

TO DECORATE:

250 ml/1 cup double/heavy cream

1 tablespoon icing/confectioners'
sugar, sifted

1/2 teaspoon vanilla bean powder
or 1 teaspoon pure vanilla extract

100 g/31/2 oz. pistachios finely
chopped

*40 x 30-cm/16 x 12-inch Swiss roll/
jelly roll pan, greased and lined*

*20 x 12 x 9-cm/8 x 5 x 31/2-inch
loaf pan*

SERVES 8–10

Preheat the oven to 180°C (350°F) Gas 4.

Begin by preparing the pistachio sponge. In a large mixing bowl, whisk together the eggs and caster/granulated sugar for about 5 minutes using an electric mixer until very thick and creamy.

Sift together the flour and baking powder and very gently fold into the egg mixture with the finely chopped pistachios. Spoon the mixture into the Swiss roll/jelly roll pan and bake for 15–20 minutes until the sponge feels just firm and is lightly golden brown. Turn the sponge out onto a sheet of baking parchment and cover with a clean damp kitchen towel and leave until cool. Remove the towel and lining paper.

For the marquise, melt the chocolate in a heatproof bowl resting over a pan of simmering water. Whisk the butter and half of the sugar together. Add the cocoa powder and whisk in. In a separate bowl whisk together the remaining sugar and egg yolks until very light and creamy. Whisk the melted chocolate and the butter mixture into the egg mixture. In a separate bowl, whip the double/heavy cream to stiff peaks then gently fold into the chocolate mixture.

Cut a rectangle of sponge that is the width of the long side of the loaf pan and long enough to cover the base and both sides of the pan with about an extra 2.5 cm/1 inch of cake up above the top of the pan sides. Line the loaf pan with a double layer of clingfilm/plastic wrap and then press the cut cake inside. Cut the remaining cake into rectangles of cake the same size as the base of the loaf pan. If you do not have enough cake to cut whole slices, you can patch pieces together in the pan as this will not be visible.

Spoon one-third of the marquise into the cake-lined pan and then cover with a layer of cake. Repeat to make two more layers of marquise and sponge.

Fold the overhanging cake edges over the cake to make a base, and then wrap the whole pan tightly in several layers of clingfilm/plastic wrap to hold in place. Chill in the refrigerator overnight.

When you are ready to serve the cake, place the double/heavy cream, icing/confectioners' sugar and vanilla in a mixing bowl and whip to stiff peaks. Lift the marquise from the pan and remove the clingfilm/plastic wrap. Place on a serving plate and then spread a thin layer of cream over the top, sides and end of the cake. Sprinkle the cream-covered surfaces with finely chopped pistachios. Serve straight away or store in the refrigerator for up to 2 days.

Stripy passion fruit and chocolate panna cotta

I was first introduced to the unusual combination of chocolate and passion fruit when I worked with the wonderful chef Hélène Darroze in Paris. I had a magical time in her kitchen and was shown how to make chocolate candy floss/cotton candy and delicious panna cotta. This dessert – a pretty, layered chocolate and passion fruit panna cotta – is a match made in heaven, inspired by the beautiful desserts in Hélène's restaurant. The panna cotta will store for up to 3 days in the refrigerator so makes a great prepare-ahead dessert for dinner parties.

FOR THE PASSION FRUIT PANNA COTTA:

2 sheets of leaf gelatine (platinum grade available in supermarkets)

225 ml/scant 1 cup double/heavy cream

100 g/$^1/_2$ cup caster/granulated sugar

4 ripe passion fruit

225 ml/scant 1 cup low-fat natural/plain yogurt

FOR THE CHOCOLATE PANNA COTTA:

100 g/3$^1/_2$ oz. plain/semisweet chocolate

2 sheets of leaf gelatine (platinum grade available in supermarkets)

225 ml/scant 1 cup double/heavy cream

60 g/5 tablespoons caster/granulated sugar

225 ml/scant 1 cup low-fat natural/plain yogurt

TO SERVE:

4 ripe passion fruit

8 dariole moulds or ramekins

SERVES 8

Begin by preparing the passion fruit panna cotta. Soak the gelatine in cold water for a few minutes until softened. Heat the cream and the sugar and simmer until the sugar has melted. Bring to the boil and then remove from the heat. Squeeze the water from the gelatine and add the gelatine to the pan and whisk in until the gelatine has melted. Cut the passion fruit in half and scoop the contents into a fine-mesh sieve/strainer resting over a large bowl. Rub and press the fruit with the back of a spoon to release all the flesh and juice, discarding the seeds. Stir the yogurt into the passion fruit, then pour in the warm cream and whisk well. Divide the cream between the eight moulds, half-filling each of them. Leave to cool and then transfer to the refrigerator and leave to set for 4 hours.

For the chocolate panna cotta, break the chocolate into pieces and place in a heatproof bowl over a pan of simmering water and simmer until melted. Set aside, keeping warm, while you prepare the cream. Soak the gelatine in cold water until softened. Heat the cream and the sugar and simmer until the sugar has melted. Bring to the boil and then remove from the heat. Squeeze the water from the gelatine and add the gelatine to the pan and whisk in until the gelatine has melted. Stir in the melted chocolate and yogurt and whisk well. Leave to cool, then pour into the moulds on top of the set passion fruit layer. Leave to set for 4 hours until firm.

When you are ready to serve, slide a sharp knife around the sides of each mould. Dip the bases of the moulds into hot water to release the panna cotta and then invert onto your serving plates. The panna cotta should slide out. If they do not, dip in the hot water for a few further seconds. Spoon the flesh from half a passion fruit on top of each panna cotta and around the base to serve.

fruity layers

Here you will find some fresh and fruity treats including Pineapple
Mint Parfait, Peaches and Cream Pavlova and a decadent Raspberry
Chambord Trifle, all with the prettiest of layers. You will find that trifles
are the perfect prepare-ahead desserts because the fruity flavours taste
best if given time to infuse. This chapter also contains a simple
Rainbow Fruit Salad with Champagne Syrup and an impressive
Puff Pastry Strawberry Ring, made with rings of crisp pastry layered
up with strawberries and cream – the ideal centrepiece
for a summer garden party.

Rhubarb and custard sundae

This is a perfect summer's day dessert with pretty pale pink and yellow layers. The rhubarb crisp decoration gives the dessert an elegant finish. Rather than individual servings, you can also make this as a big-bowl dessert.

FOR THE POACHED RASPBERRIES:

250 g/9 oz. fresh raspberries

80 g/6¹/2 tablespoons caster/granulated sugar

FOR THE BAKED RHUBARB:

800 g/1³/4 lbs. rhubarb, trimmed

2 tablespoons caster/granulated sugar

¹/2 teaspoon vanilla bean powder or 1 teaspoon pure vanilla extract

TO ASSEMBLE:

300 ml/1¹/4 cups double/heavy cream

500 g/1 lb. 2 oz. mascarpone cheese

200 g/7 oz. sponge finger biscuits

600 ml/2¹/2 cups ready-made vanilla custard

baking sheet, lined with a silicon mat or baking parchment

8 small glass dishes

SERVES 8

Begin by preparing the poached raspberries. Place the raspberries, caster/granulated sugar and 80 ml/5¹/2 tablespoons water in a saucepan and simmer for about 5 minutes until the raspberries are soft. Set aside to cool.

Preheat the oven to 180°C (350°F) Gas 4.

Reserve 3 sticks of the trimmed rhubarb and chop the remainder into 4-cm/1¹/2-inch pieces. Place the rhubarb in an ovenproof dish with 2 tablespoons caster/granulated sugar and 1 tablespoon water and sprinkle over the vanilla. Bake for 20–25 minutes until the rhubarb is just soft, stirring half way through cooking. Tip into a bowl and leave to cool.

Using a swivel peeler, peel long ribbons of the reserved rhubarb sticks. Place in a saucepan with 2 tablespoons of the raspberry juice from the poached raspberries and simmer for 1–2 minutes until just soft. Place the ribbons on the lined baking sheet and twist into pretty patterns. Leave in a warm place to dry overnight or bake in the oven on its lowest setting for about 1 hour or until the rhubarb is dried and crisp.

In a mixing bowl, whisk together the double/heavy cream, mascarpone and the cooled poached raspberries and remaining juice until the mixture is thick.

To assemble the sundaes, place the sponge finger biscuits over the base of the dishes, breaking the biscuits in half if your dishes are small. Divide half of the rhubarb between the dishes, spooning over a little of the cooking juices. Top with a large spoon of the raspberry mousse and top with a little custard.

Repeat the layers again, finishing with a little custard. Leave to chill in the refrigerator for 3 hours or overnight.

When you are ready to serve, decorate the top with the rhubarb ribbons. Do not put them on earlier as they will soften. These desserts will keep for up to 3 days stored in the refrigerator.

Queen of puddings

This is an old English pudding which has very humble ingredients. Stale bread and eggs are not the most appealing combination but when baked together with jam/jelly and topped with fluffy meringue, this makes a pretty layered dessert for everyone to enjoy. This version is flavoured with orange and raspberry and has a delicious hot fruit sauce to serve on the side.

FOR THE PUDDING:

225 g/8 oz. breadcrumbs

500 ml/2 cups double/heavy cream

500 ml/2 cups milk

grated zest of 2 oranges

100 g/1/2 cup soft dark brown sugar

60 g/1/2 stick butter, melted

4 UK large/US extra-large egg yolks

FOR THE MERINGUE:

4 UK large/US extra-large egg whites

225 g/generous 1 cup caster/granulated sugar

1/2 teaspoon vanilla bean powder or seeds of 1 vanilla pod/bean

FOR THE JAM/JELLY LAYER:

1 jar good-quality raspberry jam/jelly (approx. 370 g/13 oz.)

freshly squeezed juice of 1 large orange

FOR THE SAUCE:

250 g/9 oz. raspberry jam/jelly

juice of 1 large orange

30 g/2 tablespoons butter

large ovenproof dish, greased

piping/pastry bag, fitted with a large round nozzle/tip

SERVES 8

Place the breadcrumbs in a large mixing bowl and pour over the cream and milk. Add the orange zest, brown sugar and melted butter and stir everything together. Beat the egg yolks and whisk in. Pour the mixture into the ovenproof dish and leave to stand for 30 minutes to allow the breadcrumbs to absorb the liquid.

Preheat the oven to 180°C (350°F) Gas 4.

Bake for 25–30 minutes in the preheated oven until the sponge is golden brown.

While the sponge is cooking, prepare the meringue. Whisk the egg whites to stiff peaks, then fold in the sugar a tablespoonful at a time. Whisk in the vanilla.

For the jam/jelly layer, whisk together the raspberry jam/jelly and orange juice.

Once the sponge has cooked, remove it from the oven and pour the jam/jelly mixture over. Spoon the meringue into the piping/pastry bag and pipe in large peaks on top of the jam/jelly, pulling the piping/pastry bag away so that the meringue forms high peaks. If you do not have a piping/pastry bag, spoon the meringue on top and swirl into decorative peaks with a fork or spatula.

Bake for a further 25–30 minutes in the preheated oven until the meringue is golden brown.

While the meringue is cooking, prepare the sauce. Heat the raspberry jam/jelly with the juice of the orange and the butter and simmer until the butter is melted. Strain through a sieve/strainer to remove the seeds, then serve warm alongside the pudding. Serve with additional pouring cream if you wish. The pudding should be served straight away.

Raspberry Chambord trifle

FOR THE JELLY:

2 x 135 g packets of raspberry jelly (UK) or 2 x 3 oz. packets of Jello (US) (or sufficient to make 1 litre/quart of jelly/Jello)

200 g/7 oz. frozen raspberries

freshly squeezed juice of 1 large orange

FOR THE CAKE:

115 g/generous 1/2 cup caster/ granulated sugar

115 g/1 stick butter, softened

2 UK large/US extra-large eggs

85 g/2/3 cup self-raising/self-rising flour

60 g/generous 1/2 cup ground almonds

100 g/3 1/2 oz. fresh raspberries

FOR THE RASPBERRY CREAM:

250 g/9 oz. mascarpone cheese

300 ml/1 1/4 cups crème fraîche or sour cream

1 tablespoon icing/confectioners' sugar, sifted

200 g/7 oz. frozen raspberries, defrosted

TO ASSEMBLE:

2–3 tablespoons Chambord raspberry liqueur

150 g/5 1/2 oz. frozen raspberries, defrosted

250 ml/1 cup double/heavy cream

1/2 teaspoon vanilla bean powder or 1 teaspoon pure vanilla extract

1 tablespoon icing/confectioners' sugar, sifted

freeze-dried raspberries, to sprinkle

20-cm/8-inch round cake pan, greased and lined

large glass dish

SERVES 8–10

Chambord is a delicious raspberry liqueur and it was the inspiration for this dessert – it is one of my friend Julia's favourite drinks and she asked for this special recipe to be included. If you want to make an alcohol-free version, simply drizzle the sponges with a little raspberry coulis or syrup instead – the results will be just as good. I use both frozen and fresh raspberries for this recipe. When frozen raspberries have defrosted they release a lovely raspberry juice, so are perfect to add to the jelly and raspberry cream to give added colour and flavour. However, when making the raspberry almond sponge use fresh raspberries as you do not want the cake to be too soggy from the additional moisture contained in the frozen berries.

Make up the jelly/Jello following the packet instructions. Add the frozen raspberries to the jelly/Jello with the orange juice and pour into the dish. Once cool, place in the refrigerator overnight to set.

Preheat the oven to 180°C (350°F) Gas 4.

To prepare the cake, whisk together the caster/granulated sugar and butter until light and creamy. Add the eggs, one at a time, beating after each egg is added. Sift in the flour, add the ground almonds and fold in gently. Spoon the mixture into the prepared cake pan and place the raspberries on top, distributing them evenly. Bake for 35–40 minutes until the cake is firm and springs back to your touch (the raspberries will have sunk into the sponge). Turn out onto a rack to cool.

For the raspberry cream, place the mascarpone and crème fraîche in a mixing bowl with the icing/confectioners' sugar and whisk together. Add the defrosted raspberries and any juices from the packet and whisk in. The cream will thicken.

Cut the cake into slices and place in a layer on top of the jelly in the trifle bowl. Depending on the size of your dish you may not need all of the cake. Drizzle the cake with the Chambord liqueur and sprinkle over the 150 g/5 1/2 oz. of defrosted raspberries and any juices. Spoon the raspberry cream on top in an even layer. Whip the double/heavy cream to stiff peaks with the icing/confectioners' sugar and vanilla, and then spoon over the raspberry cream. Sprinkle with the freeze- dried raspberries. Store in the refrigerator until you are ready to serve. This dessert will keep for up to 3 days covered in the refrigerator, although only put the freeze-dried raspberries on just before serving.

Boodle's orange friand pudding

Boodle's Club in London's St. James's Street was founded in 1764 and this luscious dessert has been on their menu for many years. It contains two of my favourite things – deliciously light vanilla-scented friand cakes and a tangy citrus cream. I used to make this recipe regularly for dinner parties when I was at university, something I had completely forgotten until reminded of it by my lovely friend Fay Tinnion – thank you Fay!

FOR THE FRIANDS:

100 g/7 tablespoons butter

100 g/1 cup ground almonds

120 g/generous 1/2 cup caster/granulated sugar

50 g/6 tablespoons plain/all-purpose flour, sifted

1/2 teaspoon vanilla bean powder or 1 teaspoon pure vanilla extract

3 UK large/US extra-large egg whites

FOR THE BOODLE LAYER:

3 oranges

2 lemons

100 g/1/2 cup caster/granulated sugar

600 ml/2 1/2 cups double/heavy cream

FOR DECORATION:

1 orange

2 tablespoons caster/granulated sugar

10 friand moulds or a 12-hole muffin pan, greased

large trifle dish

SERVES 8

Preheat the oven to 180°C (350°F) Gas 4.

Begin by preparing the friands. Heat the butter in a saucepan until melted, then leave to cool. Place the ground almonds, sugar, flour and vanilla in a mixing bowl and stir together. Mix in the melted butter.

In a separate mixing bowl, whisk the egg whites to stiff peaks. Add one-third of the egg whites to the almond mixture and fold through to loosen the batter. Then fold through the remainder of the egg whites. It is important to fold gently so that you do not knock all of the air out of the egg whites as there is no raising/rising agent in the friand batter.

Spoon the batter into the moulds or into 10 of the holes in the muffin pan and bake in the preheated oven for 15–20 minutes until the cakes are firm to touch and golden brown on top. Loosen the cakes with a sharp knife, sliding it around the edge of the mould or pan and turn out onto a cooling rack. Leave to cool completely.

Press the cakes into the base of the trifle dish.

For the boodle topping, remove the zest of both the lemons and one of the oranges and place in a mixing bowl with the juice of all of the oranges and lemons. Add the caster/granulated sugar and leave for about 10 minutes until the sugar dissolves, stirring occasionally.

Place the cream in a mixing bowl and pour in one-third of the citrus juice and zest mixture. While still whisking, pour in the remainder of the juice. Do not worry if the mixture starts to curdle – keep pouring in the juice and it will recombine. Whisk until the mixture holds soft peaks. This will not take very long. Spoon the orange cream into the trifle bowl, making sure that all of the friands are covered. Leave in the refrigerator overnight. Some of the citrus juice will separate out from the cream and will soak into the cakes.

For the decoration, zest long strips of the orange peel. Squeeze the juice from the orange into a saucepan. Add the sugar and simmer until the sugar has dissolved. Add the zest to the pan and simmer for 5 minutes until soft. Leave the zest to cool in the syrup. When you are ready to serve, drain the zest from the syrup and place on top of the boodle. This dessert is best eaten within 2 days.

Strawberry shortcake layer mousses

These layered mousses are inspired by the classic American favourite strawberry shortcakes. With a tangy lemon and vanilla-scented strawberry mousse layered with buttery shortcake biscuit/cookie crumbs and slices of ripe strawberries, this is a perfect dinner party dessert for summer evenings.

FOR THE MOUSSE:

3 sheets of leaf gelatine (platinum grade available in supermarkets)

400 g/14 oz. ripe strawberries, hulled and sliced

100 g/½ cup caster/granulated sugar

½ teaspoon vanilla bean powder or vanilla bean paste

juice and zest of 1 lemon

300 ml/1¼ cups double/heavy cream

80 g/scant ⅔ cup cream cheese

FOR THE CHEESECAKE CRUMB LAYER:

200 g/7 oz. shortcake biscuits/cookies

100 g/7 tablespoons butter

TO ASSEMBLE:

300 g/10½ oz. ripe strawberries

150 ml/⅔ cup double/heavy cream

6 pretty glasses

2 piping/pastry bags, fitted with large round nozzles/tips

SERVES 6

Soak the gelatine leaves in cold water until soft. This will take about 5 minutes.

Place the strawberries, sugar, vanilla, lemon juice and lemon zest in a saucepan with 100 ml/⅓ cup water and heat for about 5 minutes until the strawberries are very soft. Pass the mixture through a sieve/strainer, pressing down on the strawberries firmly with the back of a spoon so that they become a fruit purée. Discard any strawberries remaining in the sieve/strainer. Squeeze the water out of the gelatine leaves and add to the warm strawberry syrup. Stir until dissolved, then pass through the sieve/strainer again to remove any undissolved gelatine pieces. Leave to cool. Whisk the double/heavy cream and cream cheese together and then whisk in the strawberry syrup.

Blitz the shortcake biscuits/cookies to fine crumbs. Melt the butter and then stir into the crumbs to ensure they are all coated.

To assemble, reserve 3 strawberries for decoration, then hull and slice the rest. Place a large spoonful of crumbs into the base of each glass and then top each with several slices of the strawberries. Spoon the strawberry mousse into one piping/pastry bag and pipe a generous swirl of mousse into the glasses. Repeat with a second layer of crumbs, strawberries and mousse and then leave to chill in the refrigerator for 3 hours or ideally overnight.

To serve, whip the 150 ml/⅔ cup double/heavy cream to stiff peaks and spoon into the second piping/pastry bag and pipe small swirls of cream around the edge of each mousse. Decorate each glass with a reserved strawberry half to finish.

Rainbow fruit salad with Champagne syrup

Fruit salad, while fresh and healthy, is perhaps not the most exciting of desserts. However this is a pimped-up version – fruits layered in pretty glasses laced with a Champagne syrup and served with elderflower thins on the side. The fruits listed below are suggestions only and you can use any fruits that you like – for a winter version you could opt for plums, blackberries and pomegranate. The actual quantities of fruit needed will depend on the size of your glasses. Alternatively, you can make a large layered fruit salad in a trifle bowl which would look beautiful. Serve with the crisp thin biscuits/cookies on the side for added texture and crunch, although if you are short of time, store-bought shortbread would work, too.

FOR THE FRUIT SALAD:

250 g/9 oz. strawberries

1 ripe mango

2 handfuls green and red grapes

120 g/4 oz. raspberries

2 nectarines

3 kiwi fruit

FOR THE SYRUP:

300 ml/1¼ cups Champagne or sparkling wine

2 tablespoons elderflower cordial

100 g/½ cup caster/granulated sugar

FOR THE ELDERFLOWER THINS:

50 ml/3½ tablespoons elderflower cordial

50 g/3½ tablespoons butter

150 g/1 cup plus 2 tablespoons plain/all-purpose flour, sifted

100 g/¾ cup icing/confectioners' sugar, sifted

1 UK large/US extra-large egg white

2 tablespoons finely chopped pistachios

6 elegant glasses

2 baking sheets, lined with silicon mats or baking parchment

SERVES 6

Begin by preparing the syrup as this needs to chill before being poured over the fruit. Heat the Champagne, elderflower and sugar in a saucepan until the sugar has dissolved and you have a thin syrup. Do not boil the syrup as this will evaporate the alcohol. Leave to cool and then chill in the refrigerator for at least 3 hours.

Chop all of the fruit into small pieces, keeping each type of fruit in a separate pile. In each glass, layer up the fruit in alternate layers of colours. Place the glasses in the refrigerator to chill for at least an hour.

For the elderflower thins, preheat the oven to 180°C (350°F) Gas 4. Place the cordial in a mixing bowl. Melt the butter, leave to cool slightly and then add to the cordial. Add the flour, icing/confectioners' sugar and egg white and whisk for a few minutes with an electric mixer until you have a smooth paste. Place spoonfuls of the paste on the prepared baking sheets, a distance apart and then spread out thinly using a palette knife or spoon to make rounds about 8 cm/3 inches in diameter. The batter should make about 18 biscuits/cookies. Sprinkle with the finely chopped pistachios and bake for 10–14 minutes until lightly golden brown.

When you are ready to serve, pour a little of the syrup over each glass and serve straight away with some of the elderflower thins on the side.

Puff pastry strawberry ring

This dessert looks spectacular, similar to the French classic croquembouche, but is actually far simpler to prepare and tastes light and delicious. If you prefer, you can make small individual portions, or for a special celebration, you can increase the number of puff pastry rings and make a giant tower instead.

500 g/1 lb. 2 oz. all-butter puff pastry

1 UK large/US extra-large egg, beaten

1 tablespoon caster/granulated sugar

300 ml/1¼ cups double/heavy cream

2 tablespoons icing/confectioners' sugar

seeds of ½ vanilla pod/bean or 1 teaspoon pure vanilla extract

400 g/14 oz. strawberries, hulled and sliced

plain/all-purpose flour, for dusting

icing/confectioners' sugar for dusting

large baking sheet (or 2 smaller baking sheets), lined with silicon mats or baking parchment

8-cm/3-inch round cookie cutter

SERVES 6

Preheat the oven to 200°C (400°F) Gas 6.

On a flour-dusted surface, roll out the pastry very thinly into a large rectangle using a rolling pin. Cut out one large disc of pastry using a 25-cm/10-inch plate as a template, cutting round it with a sharp knife. Using the rolling pin to help lift, transfer the pastry disc to the baking sheet. Next, cut out two smaller discs of pastry using 14-cm/5½-inch and 18-cm/7-inch plates as templates. Transfer both discs of pastry to the baking sheet(s) and cut a hole in the centre of each of the two smaller pastry discs using the 8-cm/3-inch round cutter. Discard one of the cut-out circles and place the other on the baking sheet(s). (You should have 25-cm/10-inch and 8-cm/3-inch round discs of pastry and 14-cm/5½-inch and 18-cm/7-inch rings.)

Brush the top of the pastry with a little of the beaten egg using a pastry brush and sprinkle with a little caster/granulated sugar. Bake in the preheated oven for 25–30 minutes until the pastry is crisp and golden brown and has risen. Leave on the baking sheet(s) to cool.

When you are ready to serve, in a clean mixing bowl, whisk the double/heavy cream, icing/confectioners' sugar and vanilla together to stiff peaks.

Place the largest disc of pastry on your serving plate and spread about half of the cream over and cover with some of the strawberry slices. Carefully spread a little cream around the top of the largest ring of pastry (taking care as it is fragile) and then place on top of the strawberry-covered disc. Decorate with strawberries. Repeat these steps with the smaller ring. Top the ring with cream and strawberries and place the small pastry disc on top. Dust the whole cake with icing/confectioners' sugar and serve immediately, cutting the cake into slices with a sharp knife. The cake is best eaten on the day it is assembled although you can cook the pastry the day before if you wish.

Peaches and cream pavlova

This light and fragrant dessert is one of my favourites. It has three lovely layers of meringue sandwiching a peach cream mousse, with a naughty kick of amaretto. The meringue layers are topped with toasted almonds and the final addition to this yummy dessert is slices of peaches poached in a little more amaretto. It is peach-tastic!

FOR THE PAVLOVAS:

5 UK large/US extra-large egg whites

280 g/scant 1½ cups caster/granulated sugar

½ teaspoon vanilla bean powder

orange food colouring gel or paste

40 g/½ cup flaked/slivered almonds

FOR THE PEACH CREAM:

2 ripe peaches

30 g/2 tablespoons butter

75 ml/5 tablespoons amaretto liqueur

600 ml/2½ cups double/heavy cream

FOR THE POACHED PEACHES:

4 ripe peaches

75 ml/5 tablespoons amaretto liqueur

1 tablespoon caster/granulated sugar

TO ASSEMBLE:

icing/confectioners' sugar, for dusting

roasting dish
3 baking sheets, lined with silicon mats or baking parchment

SERVES 8–10

Begin by preparing the peach purée for the peach cream. Preheat the oven to 180°C (350°F) Gas 4.

Cut both the peaches in half and remove the stones/pits. Place in a roasting dish with the butter and amaretto and bake for about 30 minutes until the peaches are soft. Leave to cool then blitz to a purée in a blender. Chill until you are ready to make the peach cream.

Reduce the oven temperature to 140°C (275°F) Gas 1.

For the meringues, whisk the egg whites to stiff peaks, then add the caster/granulated sugar very gradually, a tablespoonful at a time. Whisk in the vanilla powder. Spread one-third of the meringue into a circle on a lined baking sheet about 20 cm/8 inches in diameter.

Colour the remaining meringue with a few drops of orange food colouring. You only need a drop or two as you want your meringue to be a pretty peach colour rather than a vibrant orange. Do not use water-based colouring as this will affect the meringue. Spread half of the orange meringue out into a circle on one of the remaining baking sheets and the other half of the meringue on the other baking sheet. All three meringues should be the same size. Sprinkle the meringues with the flaked/slivered almonds.

Bake the meringues for about 1½ hours until crisp. Leave to cool.

For the poached peaches, place the 4 whole peaches into a saucepan and cover with water. Add the amaretto and sugar to the pan and simmer the peaches for about 20 minutes until soft. Remove from the heat and drain the peaches. Split the skin of each peach with a sharp knife and peel away the skins. Discard the skins and stones/pits, cutting the peaches into slices.

To finish the peach cream, whip the cream to stiff peaks and fold in the peach purée in a ripple effect.

When you are ready to serve, place one of the peach-coloured meringues on a serving plate. Spread with half of the peach mousse and top with half of the peach slices. Cover with the uncoloured meringue. Top with the remaining cream and peach slices and then top with the final peach meringue.

Dust lightly with icing/confectioners' sugar and serve straight away. Store any leftovers in the refrigerator. It is best eaten on the day it is made but will keep for up to 2 days in the refrigerator.

Pineapple mint parfait

Fresh pineapple has such a tropical taste but when roasted it takes on a whole new dimension. Mint and pineapple are a great combination. When paired with white chocolate in this recipe, you get one yummy dessert. Layered in glasses with dried pineapple crisps for decoration, this dessert will bring memories of sunshine and hot holiday days.

FOR THE PINEAPPLE:

1 large ripe pineapple

2 tablespoons dark muscovado sugar

1 tablespoon freshly chopped mint

FOR THE MINT WHITE CHOCOLATE CREAM:

1 heaped tablespoon muscovado sugar

1 tablespoon freshly chopped mint

100 g/3½ oz. white chocolate

300 ml/1¼ cups double/heavy cream

baking sheet, lined with a silicon mat or baking parchment

mandoline (optional)

6 sundae glasses

SERVES 6

Preheat the oven to 140°C (275°F) Gas 1.

Peel the skin from the pineapple using a sharp knife and then cut out the eyes. Using a mandoline or a very sharp knife cut 6 very thin discs of pineapple. Place on the prepared baking sheet and bake in the preheated oven for 1–2 hours until the pineapple slices are crisp and dried. Watch carefully towards the end of cooking as they can turn brown quite quickly if you are not careful. The actual amount of cooking time will depend on how thick you cut your slices and how juicy your pineapple is. Leave to cool.

Increase the oven temperature to 180°C (350°F) Gas 4.

Chop the remainder of the pineapple (it should be about two-thirds of the pineapple), removing and discarding the core. Place in a heatproof bowl. In a pestle and mortar crush together the muscovado sugar with the mint leaves, so all the mint leaves are incorporated into the sugar. Sprinkle the mint sugar over the pineapple and bake in the preheated oven for about 20 minutes until the pineapple just starts to caramelize. Remove from the oven, stir well and leave to cool.

For the cream, place the muscovado sugar and mint in a saucepan with 60 ml/¼ cup water and simmer until the sugar has dissolved and you have a thin syrup. Leave to cool for about 10 minutes and then strain away the mint. Melt the white chocolate in a heatproof bowl resting over a saucepan of simmering water. Stir the mint syrup into the melted white chocolate. Leave to cool.

In a mixing bowl, whisk together the double/heavy cream and melted mint chocolate mixture until the cream holds stiff peaks. To assemble, place layers of the mint cream and roasted pineapple in sundae glasses until the glasses are full. Decorate each with a dried pineapple crisp and serve straight away.

Layered plum crunch

When I was little we would go to my grandparents' house for a roast Sunday lunch and for dessert my Grandma would often serve warm roasted plums, sweetened with a little sugar and flavoured with cinnamon. This scrumptious layered dessert is inspired by that childhood memory and features layers of mascarpone cream, roasted plums and buttery crumbly crunch.

FOR THE ROASTED PLUMS:

1.2 kg/2^3/$_4$ lbs. ripe red plums

100 g/^{1}/$_2$ cup caster/granulated sugar

1 teaspoon ground cinnamon

1 teaspoon pure vanilla extract or ^{1}/$_2$ teaspoon vanilla bean powder

FOR THE CRUNCH:

200 g/1^3/$_4$ sticks butter

300 g/2^1/$_4$ cups self-raising/self-rising flour

150 g/^{3}/$_4$ cup caster/granulated sugar

FOR THE CREAM LAYER:

500 ml/2 cups mascarpone

600 ml/2^1/$_2$ cups double/heavy cream

3 tablespoons icing/confectioners' sugar, sifted

large baking sheet, lined with a silicon mat or baking parchment

large glass dish

SERVES 10

Preheat the oven to 180°C (350°F) Gas 4.

Cut the plums in half and remove the stones/pits. Sprinkle with the caster/granulated sugar, ground cinnamon and vanilla and pour over 125 ml/^{1}/$_2$ cup of water. Bake in the preheated oven for 30–40 minutes depending on the ripeness of the plums until they are soft, then leave to cool. Keep the oven on for cooking the crunch.

Prepare the crunch mixture while the plums are cooking. In a large mixing bowl rub the butter into the self-raising/self-rising flour until the mixture resembles fine breadcrumbs and comes together when you press the mixture with your fingertips. Mix in the caster/granulated sugar. Spread out on the baking sheet and bake for 10–15 minutes until golden brown, stirring halfway through to ensure that the crumble does not burn. Pour into a dish and leave to cool.

When the crunch and plums are completely cool, whisk together the mascarpone cheese, double/heavy cream and icing/confectioners' sugar until thick.

To assemble, sprinkle one-quarter of the crunch mixture over the base of the glass dish. Top with one-third of the plums and spread out evenly. Cover with one-third of the cream mixture and spread out in an even layer. Repeat for two more layers, ending with an extra layer of crunch on top. Chill in the refrigerator for 3 hours. This dessert will store for up to 3 days in the refrigerator.

indulgent layers

Discover decadent desserts such as the rich Chocolate Peanut Butter and Jelly Terrine, Toasted Marshmallow Espresso Cake or Pistachio Profiterole Stack – all perfect to serve at the end of a special dinner. Or why not try the naughty Caramel Brownie Cheesecake with interleaving layers of brownie, salted caramel cheesecake and brownie cheesecake? This chapter also contains one of my favourite desserts, a Toblerone Tiramisu. It is one I have been making for over 20 years and it never fails to impress. A twist on the classic Italian version, amaretto and chunks of nougat-filled chocolate are layered up with chocolate muffins and clouds of sweetened mascarpone cream.

Pistachio profiterole stack

This pretty tower of profiteroles is perfect for a celebration. Filled with a light pistachio Chantilly cream and topped with glossy shades of pastel fondant icing/frosting, it makes a spectacular centrepiece.

FOR THE CHOUX BUNS/ CREAM PUFFS:

100 g/7 tablespoons butter, cut into cubes

pinch of salt

1 teaspoon caster/granulated sugar

130 g/1 cup plain/all-purpose flour, sifted twice to remove any lumps and to add as much air as possible

4 UK large/US extra-large eggs, whisked

FOR THE PISTACHIO CHANTILLY FILLING:

100 g/3^1/$_2$ oz. shelled pistachios

2 tablespoons icing/confectioners' sugar, sifted

600 ml/2^1/$_2$ cups double/heavy cream

FOR THE ICING/FROSTING:

500 g/3^2/$_3$ cups fondant icing/ confectioners' sugar, sifted

green and pink food colouring gel or paste

2 piping/pastry bags fitted with round nozzles/tips

2 baking sheets, lined with silicon mats or baking parchment

SERVES 10

Heat the butter in a saucepan with 300 ml/1^1/$_4$ cups water, salt and sugar until the butter has melted. As soon as the butter has melted, shoot in the sifted flour all in one go and remove the saucepan from the heat. Beat the mixture very hard with a wooden spoon until the dough forms a ball and no longer sticks to the sides of the saucepan. Leave to cool for about 5 minutes – this cooling stage is important. Beat the whisked eggs into the pastry a little at a time using a wooden spoon until a sticky paste, which holds its shape when the spoon is lifted, forms.

Preheat the oven to 200°C (400°F) Gas 6. Sprinkle a little water into the bottom of the oven. This will create steam which will help the pastry to rise.

Spoon the pastry into one of the piping/pastry bags and pipe 48 small balls (about 2.5 cm/1 inch each) onto the lined baking sheets. Pat down any peaks in the pastry using a clean wet finger. Bake in the oven for 10 minutes, then reduce the oven temperature to 180°C (350°F) Gas 4 and bake for a further 10–15 minutes until the pastry is crisp. Remove from the oven and cut a small slit into each bun to allow steam to escape. Return to the oven and cook for a further 5 minutes to make sure the buns are very crisp. Leave to cool.

Finely chop about one-fifth of the pistachios and set aside for decoration. Blitz the remainder in a food processor to a fine dust and stir in the icing/confectioners' sugar. Place the pistachio and sugar mixture into a mixing bowl with the double/heavy cream and whisk to stiff peaks. Spoon into the second piping/pastry bag. Using a sharp knife, carefully pierce a hole in the base of each bun by inserting it and then twisting the knife 180 degrees. Using the second piping/pastry bag, pipe some cream into each bun through the hole in the base.

For the icing/frosting, gradually add 3–4 tablespoons of water to the icing/confectioners' sugar and mix until you have a smooth, thick icing that is not too runny. Divide the icing into two bowls. Colour one pale green and the other pale pink with a few drops of food colouring.

Carefully dip 12 of the buns into the green icing and fix into a ring on a cake stand, securing at the base with a little icing. Fill the centre of the ring with five buns. Sprinkle the outer buns with some of the chopped pistachios. Repeat with another slightly smaller ring of buns, this time dipped in the pink icing. Repeat the layers, alternating pink and green and sprinkling each layer with pistachios. These buns are best eaten as soon as they are assembled.

Chocolate peanut butter and jelly terrine

This cake is the ultimate in kitschness, featuring the favourite childhood combination of peanut butter and jelly. Drizzle the ganache over so that the pretty stripy layers still show.

FOR THE CAKE:

5 UK large/US extra-large eggs

120 g/generous 1/2 cup caster/granulated sugar

120 g/scant 1/4 cup ground almonds

60 g/2/3 cup unsweetened cocoa powder, sifted

FOR THE BUTTERCREAM:

225 g/generous 1 cup caster/granulated sugar

4 UK large/US extra-large egg yolks

250 g/21/4 sticks butter

60 g/6 oz. plain/semisweet chocolate, melted

2 tablespoons crunchy peanut butter

FOR THE GANACHE:

150 ml/2/3 cup double/heavy cream

30 g/2 tablespoons butter

100 g/31/2 oz. plain/semisweet chocolate, broken into pieces

2 tablespoons liquid glucose

TO ASSEMBLE:

2 tablespoons raspberry jam/jelly

35 x 25-cm/14 x 10-inch deep baking pan, greased and lined

25 x 12-cm/10 x 5-inch loaf pan, lined with a triple layer of clingfilm/plastic wrap which hangs over the edges

SERVES 10

Preheat the oven to 180°C (350°F) Gas 4.

For the cake, place the eggs and caster/granulated sugar in the bowl of a stand mixer and whisk for about 5 minutes until the mixture is very thick and creamy. Alternatively you can do this using an electric hand whisk. Fold the ground almonds and cocoa powder into the egg mixture gently until incorporated. Pour the mixture into the baking pan and spread level with a spatula. Bake in the oven for 30–35 minutes until lightly golden brown on top and the cake springs back to your touch. Turn out onto a rack to cool.

For the buttercream, heat the caster/granulated sugar and 60 ml/1/4 cup water in a saucepan over a gentle heat until the sugar has dissolved, then bring to the boil and boil until the temperature reaches soft-ball stage (119°C/238°F on a sugar thermometer).

While the caramel is cooking, whisk the egg yolks in a separate bowl until light and creamy. Turn the speed down and slowly pour in the caramel. Whisk until the mixture is light and voluminous and has cooled completely. Slowly add in the butter, a spoonful at a time, whisking all the time until the butter is all incorporated. Whisk for a few minutes more until the icing/frosting is light and airy. Divide the mixture in two and fold the melted chocolate into one half and whisk the peanut butter into the other half.

Cut the cake into 4 rectangles about the size of your loaf pan. You can use any trimmings to patch gaps if there is not enough cake, as this will not matter when the cake has set. Place one of the cake slices into the lined pan and then cover with half of the chocolate buttercream, spreading it out in an even layer using a knife or spatula. Place a second cake on top and spread over the jam/jelly. Cover with all of the peanut butter buttercream. Place a third cake on top and then spread over the rest of the chocolate buttercream. Finally cover with the last cake and wrap up tightly with the clingfilm/plastic wrap. Chill in the refrigerator for about 2 hours.

For the ganache, in a saucepan heat the cream, butter, chocolate and liquid glucose and simmer until the chocolate and butter have melted and you have a smooth glossy sauce. Leave to cool.

Invert the chilled cake onto a cooling rack and place a sheet of baking parchment underneath. Carefully spoon the ganache over. Leave for about 10 minutes, then, using a spatula, transfer the cake to a serving plate and chill in the refrigerator for at least 3 hours or overnight. The cake will store for up to up to 3 days in the refrigerator.

Rich pear and chocolate trifle

Pears and chocolate are a match made in heaven and go perfectly in this yummy twist on a classic trifle (see page 20). The pears are poached in a cinnamon-honey syrup and nestled on chocolate sponge roll before being topped with a chocolate mousse and cinnamon custard. To make the chocolate curls, run the blade of a swivel peeler along the edge of a bar of chocolate. It is important that the chocolate is at room temperature and not chilled.

FOR THE WHITE CHOCOLATE CINNAMON CUSTARD:

150 ml/²/₃ cup double/heavy cream

100 ml/¹/₃ cup whole milk

100 g/3¹/₂ oz. white chocolate

1 UK large/US extra-large egg, plus 1 yolk

2 tablespoons cornflour/cornstarch, sifted

75 g/6 tablespoons caster/granulated sugar

1 teaspoon ground cinnamon

FOR THE PEARS:

7 ripe pears

1 tablespoon runny honey

1 teaspoon ground cinnamon

FOR THE CHOCOLATE MOUSSE:

200 g/7 oz. milk chocolate

3 UK large/US extra-large egg whites

50 g/¹/₄ cup caster/granulated sugar

TO ASSEMBLE:

8 chocolate mini rolls or 1 large chocolate roll

chocolate curls, to decorate

large trifle dish

SERVES 8–10

Begin by preparing the white chocolate cinnamon custard as it needs to cool before being used in the trifle. In a saucepan heat the double/heavy cream and milk and bring to the boil. Remove from the heat and add the white chocolate, broken into pieces. Whisk until the chocolate has melted. In a mixing bowl whisk together the egg, egg yolk, cornflour/cornstarch, caster/granulated sugar and ground cinnamon until thick and creamy. Pour over the hot milk mixture and whisk until it is all incorporated.

Return to the saucepan and whisk until the custard thickens, then remove from the heat and pour into a jug/pitcher or bowl. Do not leave in the saucepan otherwise the custard will over-cook and curdle. If the custard does curdle, pass through a sieve/strainer pressing down with a rubber spatula, then re-whisk the custard. Leave to cool.

Peel and core the pears. Place them in a large saucepan and cover with water. Add the honey and cinnamon to the pan and simmer for about 15–20 minutes until the pears are just soft. Drain and leave to cool.

For the chocolate mousse, break the milk chocolate into pieces and place in a heatproof bowl resting over a saucepan of simmering water and heat until the chocolate melts. In a clean dry bowl, whisk the egg whites to stiff peaks and then whisk in the caster/granulated sugar a spoonful at a time. Fold the melted chocolate into the egg whites, gently so you do not lose all the air, but making sure that all the chocolate is incorporated. Set aside until you are ready to assemble the trifle.

To assemble, cut the chocolate rolls in half and place in a layer over the base and lower sides of the trifle dish. Place the pears on top and then cover with the custard. Carefully spoon the chocolate mousse on top and place in the refrigerator to set for 3 hours or overnight.

To serve, decorate the top of the trifle with chocolate curls. This dessert will keep for up to 3 days in the refrigerator.

Key lime trifle

Everyone loves Key lime pie, so this bowl dessert that has all the citrusy punch of the original is sure to be a winner. It has light lime sponges and a tangy lime cream. If you cannot find lime curd, just substitute lemon curd for a lemon and lime trifle.

FOR THE SPONGES:

115 g/generous 1/2 cup caster/granulated sugar

115 g/1 stick butter, softened

2 UK large/US extra-large eggs

115 g/3/4 cup plus 2 tablespoons self-raising/self-rising flour, sifted

1 tablespoon sour cream or natural/plain yogurt

grated zest of 2 limes

FOR THE KEY LIME MOUSSE:

400-g/14-oz. can of condensed milk

freshly squeezed juice of 6 limes

300 ml/11/4 cups double/heavy cream

FOR THE COOKIE CRUMB LAYER:

300 g/101/2 oz. ginger biscuits/cookies

150 g/11/4 sticks butter, melted

FOR THE CURD:

freshly squeezed juice of 2 limes

325 g/111/2 oz. lime curd

green food colouring gel or paste (optional)

TO ASSEMBLE:

300 ml/11/4 cups double/heavy cream

75 ml/5 tablespoons coconut rum (optional)

12-hole muffin pan, lined with muffin cases

large glass dish

SERVES 8–10

Preheat the oven to 180°C (350°F) Gas 4.

For the sponges, whisk together the sugar and butter until light and creamy. Add the eggs one at a time, whisking well after each addition. Using a spatula gently fold in the flour, sour cream or yogurt and the lime zest. Spoon the mixture into the paper cases in the muffin pan and bake in the oven for 20–25 minutes until the cupcakes are firm to touch and spring back when pressed with a clean finger. Set aside to cool on a wire rack, then remove the paper cases.

For the Key lime mousse, add the condensed milk to a mixing bowl with the lime juice and whisk together. Add the double/heavy cream and whisk until the mixture starts to thicken.

For the cookie crumb layer, blitz the ginger biscuits/cookies in a food processor to fine crumbs, then stir in the melted butter until all the crumbs are coated.

For the curd, whisk the lime juice into the lime curd, adding a little green food colouring gel if you wish. This will give the trifle a fun, vibrant colour, but it is for decoration only and is not absolutely necessary.

To assemble, whip the double/heavy cream to stiff peaks. Cut the sponges in half horizontally and place half of them cut-side up in the base of the glass dish. Sprinkle over half of the rum, if using. Spoon over half of the condensed milk mixture and then cover with one-third of the cookie crumbs. Top with half of the curd. Pour over the remaining condensed milk mixture and then top with the remaining halved sponge slices, drizzling with a little more rum, if using. Cover with the rest of the lime curd and half of the remaining crumbs and then top with the whipped cream. Top with a final layer of the crumbs. Chill in the refrigerator for at least 3 hours before serving. This dessert will store for up to 3 days covered in the refrigerator.

Caramel brownie cheesecake

Everyone loves cheesecake and this stripy version looks particularly attractive. It contains interleaving layers of brownie, salted caramel cheesecake and brownie cheesecake. If you like nuts, you can add an extra crunch by including 200 g/7 oz. finely chopped pecans in the caramel cheesecake layer.

FOR THE BROWNIE:

200 g/7 oz. plain/semisweet chocolate, broken into pieces

125 g/9 tablespoons butter

3 UK large/US extra-large eggs

250 g/1¼ cups caster/granulated sugar

100 g/¾ cup plain/all-purpose flour, sifted

FOR THE CARAMEL CHEESECAKE:

360 g/13 oz. cream cheese, at room temperature

400 ml/scant 1¾ cups crème fraîche or sour cream

250 g/9 oz. salted caramel sauce

3 UK large/US extra-large eggs

1 tablespoon plain/all-purpose flour

pouring cream, to serve

23-cm/9-inch round springform cake pan, greased and lined

SERVES 10

Preheat the oven to 180°C (350°F) Gas 4.

Begin by making the brownie. Place the chocolate and butter into a heatproof bowl over a saucepan of simmering water and heat until melted. Remove from the heat and leave to cool.

In a separate mixing bowl whisk the eggs and the caster/granulated sugar together using an electric whisk for about 3–5 minutes until very light and creamy. Fold in the melted chocolate mixture and the flour.

Next make the cheesecake mixture. Place the cream cheese, crème fraîche, salted caramel sauce, eggs and flour in a mixing bowl and whisk well until the mixture is smooth. It is important that the cream cheese is at room temperature otherwise there may be lumps in the batter.

Wrap the cake pan in several layers of clingfilm/plastic wrap so that it is watertight, as the cheesecake needs to be cooked in a water bath to ensure even cooking. Pour half of the brownie mixture into the base of the cake pan and spread out in an even layer.

Add one-third of the caramel cheesecake mixture to the remaining brownie mixture and fold in.

Pour half of the remaining caramel cheesecake mixture on top of the brownie layer in the cake pan. Pour the brownie cheesecake mixture on top and spread out very gently in an even layer. Finally pour the remaining caramel cheesecake on top and spread out very gently so that you do not mix the layers. You want the cheesecake to bake with stripy layers in it.

Bake in the oven for 1–1¼ hours until the cheesecake has set but still has a slight wobble in the centre. Turn the oven temperature down slightly if the top starts to brown. Leave to cool, then chill in the refrigerator for 3 hours before serving. This cheesecake will store for up to 3 days in the refrigerator. Serve with pouring cream if you wish.

Toasted marshmallow espresso cake

This can really only be described as a spectacular centrepiece. It is three layers high and covered in a gooey toasted coffee meringue. The filling is an espresso ganache rich with butter.

FOR THE CAKES:

280 g/scant 1½ cups caster/granulated sugar

280 g/2½ sticks butter, softened

5 UK large/US extra-large eggs

280 g/2 cups self-raising/self-rising flour

1 teaspoon baking powder

1 tablespoon instant coffee granules

180 g/1 cup low-fat natural/plain yogurt

FOR THE GANACHE:

240 g/8½ oz. coffee-flavoured chocolate

115 g/1 stick butter, softened

120 g/generous ¾ cup icing/confectioners' sugar, sifted

3 UK large/US extra-large egg yolks

200 ml/generous ¾ cup double/heavy cream

50 ml/3½ tablespoons espresso coffee

FOR THE MERINGUE:

150 g/¾ cup caster/granulated sugar

60 ml/¼ cup liquid glucose

125 ml/½ cup espresso coffee

whites from 3 UK large/US extra-large eggs

3 x 20-cm/8-inch round cake pans, greased and lined

piping/pastry bag fitted with a large round nozzle/tip

chef's blow torch

SERVES 10

Preheat the oven to 180°C (350°F) Gas 4.

For the cakes, in a large mixing bowl whisk together the caster/granulated sugar and butter until light and creamy. Add the eggs, one at a time, whisking after each one is added. Sift the flour and baking powder into the mixture and fold in gently. Dissolve the coffee in a tablespoon of hot water and fold into the mixture with the yogurt.

Divide the cake batter between the three cake pans and bake in the oven for 25–30 minutes until the cakes are firm and spring back to your touch, and a knife comes out clean when inserted into the centre of one of the cakes. Turn the cakes out onto a wire rack to cool completely and remove the lining paper.

For the ganache, melt the chocolate by breaking it into pieces and placing in a heatproof bowl resting over a saucepan of simmering water. In a mixing bowl, whisk together the butter and half of the icing/confectioners' sugar until light and creamy. In a separate bowl, whisk together the egg yolks and the rest of the icing/confectioners' sugar. Fold the egg mixture into the butter mixture with the melted chocolate and beat until smooth. Place the double/heavy cream and espresso coffee in another mixing bowl and whisk to stiff peaks. Gently fold the cream into the chocolate mixture.

Spoon the ganache into the piping/pastry bag and pipe circles of ganache on top of one of the cakes. Top with a second cake and again pipe circles of ganache on top of the cake. Top with the final cake and place on a cake stand or serving plate.

For the meringue coating, simmer the sugar and liquid glucose together with the coffee until the sugar has dissolved, then bring to the boil. Using a sugar thermometer heat the syrup to 119°C/238°F (soft-ball stage). In a clean dry bowl, whisk the egg whites to stiff peaks, then add the hot sugar syrup in a small drizzle while whisking continuously. This is best done with a stand mixer, or if using a hand mixer, have someone else pour in the hot sugar syrup. Whisk for about 10–15 minutes until the meringue starts to cool.

Spread the meringue over the top and sides of the cake. Toast the meringue with a blow torch and serve straight away. This cake is best eaten on the day it is made.

Layered crème brûlées

One of the best things about a crème brûlée is when you tap on the top of the sugar crust and it cracks to reveal the heavenly vanilla custard below. This is my version, which also has the crunch of a buttery chocolate cookie crumb base, topped with a rich espresso ganache and a cinnamon custard. It is the kind of dessert that just makes you reach for a spoon to dig in with.

FOR THE BASE:

150 g/5½ oz. Oreo cookies

85 g/6 tablespoons butter

FOR THE GANACHE:

100 ml/⅓ cup double/heavy cream

60 ml/¼ cup espresso coffee

30 g/2 tablespoons butter

100 g/3½ oz. plain/semisweet chocolate, broken into pieces

FOR THE CUSTARD:

400 ml/scant 1¾ cups double/heavy cream

4 UK large/US extra-large egg yolks

60 g/5 tablespoons caster/granulated sugar, plus extra for sprinkling

1 teaspoon ground cinnamon

6 small glass ramekins

chef's blow torch

SERVES 6

For the base, crush the Oreo cookies to fine crumbs in a food processor or blender. In a saucepan, melt the butter and then stir it into the crumbs, mixing well so that all the crumbs are coated. Press a large spoonful of crumbs into the base of each ramekin and leave to cool.

For the ganache, place the cream and espresso coffee in a saucepan with the broken chocolate and butter and heat over a gentle heat until the chocolate and butter melt and the ganache thickens. Place a spoonful of the ganache on top of the crumbs in the ramekins and chill in the refrigerator until set.

For the custard, heat the cream and bring to the boil. While the cream is heating, whisk the egg yolks with the sugar and cinnamon until thick and creamy. Pour over the hot cream and whisk together. It is easiest to do this using a stand mixer or have someone to help you pour. Place the custard in a large heatproof bowl resting over a pan of simmering water and whisk until the custard starts to thicken. This will take about 20–25 minutes. I find this very therapeutic and I think it gives you control over the thickness of the custard. Pour the custard into the ramekins on top of the ganache and leave to cool. If you prefer, rather than whisking over the heat, you can bake the brûlées in the oven by baking for about 30–40 minutes at 180°C (350°F) Gas 4 until the custard wobbles but does not appear to be runny. Chill in the refrigerator.

When you are ready to serve, sprinkle a fine layer of caster/granulated sugar over the top of each brûlée and toast with a blow torch until caramelized. The brûlées can be kept in the refrigerator for up to 2 days, but only make the sugar layer just before serving.

Toblerone tiramisu

While Italians will probably shudder at the thought of including Toblerone in their national dessert, I love the hints of almond and honey crunch that it adds. If you are short of time you can replace the Toblerone cupcakes with store-bought sponge fingers or trifle sponges instead for equally delicious results. I hope you enjoy my take on this classic layered dessert.

FOR THE CUPCAKES:

115 g/generous ¹/₂ cup caster/granulated sugar

115 g/1 stick butter, softened

2 UK large/US extra-large eggs

100 g/³/₄ cup self-raising/self-rising flour

30 g/¹/₃ cup unsweetened cocoa powder

80 g/3 oz. Toblerone, chopped into chunks

FOR THE CREAM:

500 g/1 lb. 2 oz. mascarpone cheese

500 ml/2 cups crème fraîche or sour cream

3 tablespoons icing/confectioners' sugar, sifted

TO ASSEMBLE:

2 tablespoons instant coffee powder

150 ml/²/₃ cup amaretto liqueur

200 g/7 oz. Toblerone, chopped

unsweetened cocoa powder, for dusting

12-hole muffin pan, lined with cupcake cases

large glass bowl

SERVES 8–10

Preheat the oven to 180°C (350°F) Gas 4.

Begin by making the cupcakes. Whisk together the sugar and butter until light and creamy. Add the eggs one at a time, whisking well after each addition. Sift in the flour and cocoa powder and fold gently to incorporate. Half fill each cupcake case with the cake mixture. Divide the chunks of Toblerone between the cupcakes, placing them in the centre of each case, and then cover with a spoonful of the remaining cake batter. Bake in the oven for 20–25 minutes until the cupcakes are firm to touch and spring back when pressed with a finger. Set aside to cool, then remove the cases.

Dissolve the instant coffee in a shallow bowl with 250 ml/1 cup boiling water. Pour in the amaretto and leave to cool. While the coffee mixture is cooling, make the cream by whisking together the mascarpone, crème fraîche and icing/confectioners' sugar in a large mixing bowl.

Soak half of the cupcakes in the coffee mixture. It is best to do this one at a time as the cupcakes can become soggy if they are in the liquid too long. You want them to absorb some of the liquid but still retain their shape. Place half the cakes on the bottom of the trifle dish, pressing them down with a spoon so that the cupcakes make a layer over the bottom of the dish.

To assemble, sprinkle over half the chopped Toblerone and dust with cocoa powder using a fine-mesh sieve/strainer. Spoon half the mascarpone mixture over the top and dust with another layer of sifted cocoa powder. Soak the remaining sponges, as before, in the coffee mixture and place on top of the cocoa layer. Cover with the remaining Toblerone and dust with another cocoa layer. Spoon in the remaining mascarpone mixture and spread out in an even layer and dust with more cocoa. Chill in the fridge, preferably overnight, to enable the flavours to develop. This dessert will store for up to 3 days in the refrigerator.

Cocoa nib meringue tower

In his Islington café, Ottolenghi, who is one of my favourite chefs, serves the most incredible meringues, which billow like clouds of loveliness and are often piled high in the shop window. I can't walk past without stopping to buy one! They are the inspiration for this layered meringue dessert – the dusting of cocoa nibs on the meringue gives them an intense chocolate flavour.

FOR THE MERINGUES:

5 UK large/US extra-large egg whites

300 g/1¹/₂ cups caster/granulated sugar

100 g/3¹/₂ oz. plain/semisweet chocolate, finely grated

1 teaspoon vanilla bean powder

cocoa nibs, to grind

unsweetened cocoa powder, for dusting

FOR THE FILLING:

150 g/5¹/₂ oz. plain/semisweet chocolate

600 ml/2¹/₂ cups double/heavy cream

2 large baking sheets, lined with silicon mats or baking parchment

SERVES 8 –10

Preheat the oven to 130°C (250°F) Gas ¹/₂.

For the meringues, in a clean mixing bowl, whisk the egg whites to stiff peaks. Add the caster/granulated sugar a spoonful at a time until you have a smooth glossy meringue. Add the grated chocolate and vanilla and gently fold into the meringue with a spatula, folding only as much as is necessary just to incorporate the chocolate, taking care not to remove too much air.

On the lined baking sheets, divide the mixture into four and make four rounds of meringue but with each one being slightly smaller than the previous one. The last and smallest meringue should be made into a higher peak as this will form the top of your meringue stack. Grind cocoa nibs over the top of each meringue and dust with a little cocoa powder.

Bake the meringues for about 1–1¹/₂ hours until they are crisp. If you are baking all the meringues at the same time on two shelves, the one lower in the oven may take longer to cook. When the meringues are crisp remove from the oven and leave to cool.

For the filling, break the chocolate into pieces and place in a heatproof bowl resting over a pan of simmering water and heat until melted. Leave the chocolate until it is cool but still runny.

Place two-thirds of the cooled chocolate into a mixing bowl with the double/heavy cream and whisk to stiff peaks. Starting with the largest meringue, place it on a serving plate and spread over one-third of the cream. Cover with the next largest meringue and again cover with one-third of the cream. Repeat with the next meringue, covering with the remaining cream and then top with the smallest meringue with the highest peak to make a pretty stack. Drizzle the whole meringue stack with the remaining chocolate.

Serve straight away, or if you wish to store the meringue, keep it in the refrigerator as it contains fresh cream. The dessert will keep for up to 2 days if stored in the refrigerator.

Mocha charlotte russe

Here is an old-fashioned dessert that will simply wow your guests. Its layers of coffee jelly, rich coffee bavarois and buttery chocolate crumb base will tempt all coffee lovers!

FOR THE COFFEE JELLY/JELLO:

3 sheets of leaf gelatine (platinum grade available in supermarkets)

250 ml/1 cup freshly brewed espresso coffee (long shots of espresso rather than short ones)

60 ml/1/4 cup coffee liqueur (I love to use Patron XO Coffee Tequila for a real coffee kick)

50 g/2 oz. white chocolate chunks

FOR THE BAVAROIS:

5 sheets of leaf gelatine (platinum grade available in supermarkets)

600 ml/2 1/2 cups double/heavy cream

100 g/3 1/2 oz. plain/semisweet chocolate, broken into pieces

100 g/1/2 cup caster/granulated sugar

100 ml/1/3 cup coffee liqueur

175 g/6 oz. sponge fingers (such as boudoir)

FOR THE CRUMB BASE:

115 g/1 stick butter, melted

250 g/9 oz. Oreo cookies, blitzed to fine crumb in a blender

25-cm/10-inch round Bundt pan (it is important that this does not have a loose bottom otherwise the jelly may leak), ideally chilled in the freezer before use

SERVES 10

Begin by preparing the coffee jelly/Jello. Soak the gelatine leaves in cold water for 5 minutes until soft. Dissolve the gelatine in the hot (not boiling) coffee, stirring until it is dissolved. Whisk in the coffee liqueur and 100 ml/1/3 cup water. Pour half of the jelly/Jello into the chilled Bundt pan and chill in the refrigerator until set. This should take about 30 minutes. Keep the remaining jelly at room temperature while the jelly in the pan sets. You need it to be cold but not set. Remove the pan from the refrigerator and sprinkle over the white chocolate chunks. Pour over the remaining cooled jelly and leave to set firm. This should take about 1 hour in the refrigerator.

For the bavarois, soak the gelatine leaves in cold water for 5 minutes. Heat the double/heavy cream in a saucepan with the plain/semisweet chocolate and caster/granulated sugar until the chocolate has melted and the sugar has dissolved. Do not boil the cream. Squeeze out the water from the gelatine leaves and add to the warm chocolate cream. Whisk until melted and then pass through a fine-mesh sieve/strainer to remove any undissolved gelatine. Whisk in the coffee liqueur. Leave to cool but not set.

Place the sponge fingers around the edge of the Bundt pan, fitting them tightly without gaps on top. Pour in the chocolate cream and leave to set for 2 hours in the refrigerator. The cream will seep through the sponge fingers to make a band of cream which will stop at the top of the cream layer about half-way up the sponge fingers. When inverted, this will give the dessert a pretty layered effect.

When the bavarois has set, melt the butter and stir into the cookie crumbs, mixing well to coat. Leave to cool before spooning on top of the set cream. It is important that the cream is set so that the crumbs do not sink. Press the crumbs down gently with the back of a spoon to flatten and make the base. The sponge fingers should be slightly higher than the crumb base. Transfer to the refrigerator to set.

When the base has set, remove from the refrigerator and, using a sharp knife and working very carefully so as not to break the jelly/Jello or cream, trim the ends of the sponge fingers down to the level of the crumb base so that when you turn it out the base will be flat.

When ready to serve, fill a basin with boiling water and dip the pan in it for a few seconds. Remove from the water, place a plate on top of the pan and, holding tightly, invert the pan. The jelly should release onto the plate easily. If it doesn't, repeat the dipping stage again. Serve straight away. Leftovers should be stored in the refrigerator and eaten within 2 days.

Raspberry chiffon layer cake

This light and airy cake has luscious layers of chiffon sponge, lemon curd, whipped cream and raspberries – it makes a perfect treat. The art of a beautiful chiffon cake is adding in as much air as possible using whipped egg whites and raising agents. This sponge is made using oil, so is a great dairy-free cake if you layer with just fruit and jam/jelly, rather than the curd and cream.

FOR THE CAKE:

225 g/1¾ cups self-raising/self-rising flour

275 g/generous 1¼ cups caster/granulated sugar

1 teaspoon baking powder

6 UK large/US extra-large eggs, separated

freshly squeezed juice of 3 lemons and grated zest of 1 lemon

½ teaspoon vanilla bean powder or pure vanilla extract

150 ml/⅔ cup vegetable oil

1 teaspoon cream of tartar

FOR THE FILLING:

400 ml/scant 1¾ cups double/heavy cream

300 g/10½ oz. fresh raspberries

4 tablespoons lemon curd or lemon cheese

icing/confectioners' sugar, for dusting

25-cm/10-inch Angel cake pan or other ring cake pan, well-greased

SERVES 8–10

Preheat the oven to 180°C (350°F) Gas 4.

Sift the flour into a large mixing bowl. Add 225 g/generous 1 cup of the caster/granulated sugar and the baking powder and stir in so that everything is well mixed. Add the egg yolks, lemon juice and zest, vanilla and oil. Mix everything together well until the mixture is light and creamy.

In a separate bowl, whisk the egg whites to stiff peaks. Whisk in the cream of tartar and then add the remaining 50 g/¼ cup caster/granulated sugar, a spoonful at a time, whisking all the time to create a glossy meringue. Spoon one-third of the meringue into the flour mixture and fold in to loosen the batter. Add another third and fold in very gently. Add the remaining third and fold in. Pour the mixture into the prepared cake pan and bake for 35–40 minutes until the cake is golden brown and feels firm to touch. Remove from the oven and slide a knife around the edge and centre of the cake and leave to cool in the pan.

To assemble the cake, using a sharp bread knife, slice the cake into thirds horizontally so that you have three rings of cake. Place the bottom ring on your serving plate. To make the filling, whip the cream to stiff peaks using an electric mixer or whisk, and spoon half of the cream over the bottom cake. Top with half of the raspberries and drizzle with some of the lemon curd. Place a second ring of cake on top and repeat with the raspberries and lemon curd. Finally place the third cake on top and dust with icing/confectioners' sugar. This cake is best eaten on the day it is made but will store for up to 2 days in an airtight container in the refrigerator.

frozen layers

If you are after a chilly affair, this chapter contains icebox cakes of all shapes and sizes – from individually portioned Mini Ice Cream Cakes to a Lemon Meringue Arctic Pie to serve eight, delightfully tangy with layers of lemon curd and citrus sponge. Not all cold desserts have to be summery, though – take the Pecan Pie Ice Cream Cake served with warm toffee sauce. I would happily eat this in winter. The showstoppers in this chapter include a surprise-inside Blackcurrant Baked Alaska covered in toasted meringue, and a fabulous Chocolate and Hazelnut Bombe.

Mini ice cream cakes

For a party treat why not serve these little ice cream sandwich layer cakes, glistening with a chocolate glaze and sandwiched with ice cream. You can use any flavour ice cream you like for these cakes. I love to decorate these cakes with pretty crystallized rose petals and if you are a fan of rose creams, you could add a little rose extract to the cake batter if you wish.

FOR THE CAKE:

225 g/generous 1 cup soft dark brown sugar

225 g/2 sticks butter, softened

4 UK large/US extra-large eggs

150 g/1 cup plus 2 tablespoons self-raising/self-rising flour

30 g/$^1/_3$ cup unsweetened cocoa powder

100 g/1 cup ground almonds

2 tablespoons natural/plain yogurt

FOR THE GLAZE:

100 g/3$^1/_2$ oz. plain/semisweet chocolate, broken into pieces

1 tablespoon golden syrup or light corn syrup

15 g/1 tablespoon butter

100 ml/$^1/_3$ cup double/heavy cream

2 heaped tablespoons icing/confectioners' sugar, sifted

TO ASSEMBLE:

400 ml/scant 1$^3/_4$ cups ice cream

crystallized rose petals, to decorate

35 x 25-cm/14 x 10-inch large baking pan, greased and lined

6-cm/2$^1/_2$-inch round chef's ring or cookie cutter

MAKES 8 MINI CAKES

Preheat the oven to 180°C (350°F) Gas 4.

In a mixing bowl, whisk together the brown sugar and butter until light and creamy. Add the eggs, one at a time, whisking after each egg is added. Sift in the self-raising/self-rising flour and fold in with the cocoa powder. Fold in the ground almonds and the yogurt. Spoon the mixture into the prepared baking pan and bake in the preheated oven for 25–30 minutes until the cake is firm to touch and a knife comes out clean. Turn the cake out onto a wire rack and leave to cool completely.

When cool, remove the lining paper and place the cake on a chopping board. Using the chef's ring or cookie cutter, cut out 16 circles of cake.

For the glaze, place the chocolate, syrup, butter and cream in a saucepan and simmer over a gentle heat until the chocolate and butter have melted and you have a smooth glossy sauce. Beat in the icing/confectioners' sugar. Pass the glaze through a fine-mesh sieve/strainer to remove any lumps of icing/confectioners' sugar.

Place the cakes on a wire rack to cool with a sheet of foil or baking parchment underneath to catch any drips. While the glaze is still hot, pour it over the cakes to cover. Decorate with crystallized rose petals and leave to set.

When you are ready to serve, use the chef's ring or cookie cutter to cut out discs of ice cream the same size as the cakes. It is easiest to bring the ice cream just to room temperature for a few minutes first. Sandwich an ice cream disc between two of the cakes and serve immediately.

Ice cream cookie sandwiches

On hot summer days there is no nicer treat to serve to kids than ice cream cookie sandwiches. These are made with chocolate, cinnamon and orange – and while the recipe calls for vanilla ice cream, you can substitute chocolate ice cream, cinnamon ice cream or even a layer of orange sorbet in place of one of the ice cream layers. You may wish to wrap the cookie towers in a strip of baking parchment and tie with string/twine to make them easier to eat.

FOR THE COOKIES:

350 g/2²/₃ cups self-raising/self-rising flour, sifted

200 g/1 cup caster/granulated sugar

¹/₂ teaspoon bicarbonate of soda/baking soda

grated zest of 1 orange

1 teaspoon ground cinnamon

125 g/9 tablespoons butter, plus extra for greasing

2 tablespoons golden syrup/light corn syrup

1 UK large/US extra-large egg, lightly beaten

200 g/7 oz. plain/semisweet chocolate, chopped into chunks

100 g/²/₃ cup white chocolate chips

TO ASSEMBLE:

500 ml/2 cups good-quality vanilla ice cream

2 baking sheets, lined with silicon mats or baking parchment

8-cm/3-inch round fluted edge cookie cutter

MAKES 10 DOUBLE- DECKER COOKIES

Preheat the oven to 180°C (350°F) Gas 4.

For the cookies, stir together the flour, caster/granulated sugar, bicarbonate of soda/baking soda, orange zest and ground cinnamon in a mixing bowl. Heat the butter with the syrup until the butter has melted, cool slightly and then stir into the dry ingredients with a wooden spoon. Beat in the egg, then fold through the chocolate chunks and chocolate chips.

Place about 20 spoonfuls of the dough on the baking sheets and press down slightly with your fingers. Make sure that you leave gaps between each as the cookies will spread during cooking. Bake for about 12–15 minutes until the cookies are golden brown. Leave to cool on the baking sheets for about 10 minutes then transfer to a rack with a spatula to cool.

When you are ready to serve, press the cookie cutter into the tub of ice cream to make discs of ice cream that are slightly smaller than the size of the cookies and then sandwich between the cookies. (Simply press the cutter into the ice cream and give it a twist and the disc should come out easily.) Serve each cookie stack straight away as the ice cream will start to melt.

Knickerbocker glory

The knickerbocker glory is a pure retro dessert that never really went out of fashion. I don't know anyone who doesn't love a tall glass filled with ice cream, fruits, syrup and wafers. I like to include crushed meringue as well to give an added texture. I use frozen summer berries as these keep in a handy pack in the freezer so you can make the dessert at any time, but you can happily substitute them with fresh berries if you have them available. The combination of fruits is entirely your choice – blackberries, blueberries, strawberries and raspberries all work well.

450 g/1 lb. frozen summer fruits

100 g/$^1/_2$ cup caster/granulated sugar

$^1/_2$ teaspoon vanilla bean powder or 1 teaspoon pure vanilla extract

4 meringue nests

300 ml/1$^1/_4$ cups double/heavy cream

8 scoops good-quality vanilla ice cream

4 fresh cherries on stalks, to decorate

4 biscuit wafer tubes

4 large sundae glasses

SERVES 4

In a saucepan, heat the frozen summer fruits with the caster/granulated sugar and vanilla and simmer for about 10–15 minutes until the fruit is soft and the liquid is syrupy. Set aside and leave to cool completely.

When you are ready to serve, crush the meringues into small pieces. Whip the double/heavy cream to soft peaks in a clean mixing bowl using an electric mixer or whisk. Layer the fruit compote with some of the cooking syrup with scoops of ice cream, cream and meringue pieces in the sundae glasses.

Top with a spoonful of cream, drizzle over a few more berries and top with a whole cherry. Insert a wafer tube into each sundae and serve immediately. You may not need all of the fruit compote and its juices depending on the size of your glasses.

Chocolate and hazelnut bombe

My friend Maren loves Nutella chocolate spread and I made this dessert especially for her. Using a chocolate sponge roll to line the basin gives the bombe a pretty decorative pattern when you cut into it – a perfect case in which to nestle the chocolate-hazelnut and ice cream layers. Top with roasted hazelnuts for a delicious crunch.

FOR THE GANACHE:

50 g/2 oz. plain/semisweet chocolate

60 ml/¼ cup double/heavy cream

15 g/1 tablespoon butter

FOR THE CHOCOLATE-HAZELNUT CREAM:

250 ml/1 cup double/heavy cream

2 heaped tablespoons Nutella

40 g/1½ oz. chopped roasted hazelnuts

TO ASSEMBLE:

360 g/12½ oz. chocolate Swiss roll/jelly roll

4 scoops hazelnut or vanilla ice cream

2 meringue nests, crushed into small pieces

3 tablespoons toasted chopped hazelnuts

FOR THE CHOCOLATE SAUCE:

100 g/3½ oz. plain/semisweet chocolate

100 ml/⅓ cup double/heavy cream

2 tablespoons golden syrup/ light corn syrup

30 g/2 tablespoons butter

large pudding basin, lined with a double layer of clingfilm/plastic wrap

SERVES 8

Begin by preparing the ganache. In a saucepan heat the chocolate, double/heavy cream and butter until you have a smooth sauce. Leave to cool completely. The ganache will thicken as it cools.

For the chocolate-hazelnut cream, place the double/heavy cream and Nutella in a large mixing bowl and whisk until the cream just holds stiff peaks. Stir through the chopped roasted hazelnuts.

To assemble, cut the chocolate Swiss roll/jelly roll into slices and use to line the basin, covering the base and all the sides. When you reach the top of the dish you may need to cut the slices in half so that you can fill the gaps.

Place half of the chocolate-hazelnut cream into the basin, then add the ganache followed by a layer of the ice cream. Sprinkle over the crushed meringue and cover with the remaining chocolate-hazelnut cream. Cover the top of the basin with thin slices of any Swiss roll/jelly roll you have left over. Wrap the whole basin in several more layers of clingfilm/plastic wrap and freeze overnight. It is important that you work quickly in the above steps to ensure that the ice cream does not melt.

When you are ready to serve, make the sauce by heating the chocolate, double/heavy cream, golden syrup/light corn syrup and butter in a saucepan until the chocolate and butter have melted and you have a smooth sauce. Take the ice cream bombe from the freezer and remove the clingfilm/plastic wrap. Place on a serving plate and allow to come to room temperature for a few minutes. Cut into slices and serve with the warm chocolate sauce poured over the top and sprinkle with toasted chopped hazelnuts. The ice cream bombe will store for up to 1 month in the freezer.

Pecan pie ice cream cake

Pecan pie is a popular American dessert and is definitely one of our family favourites. This ice cream cake is topped with crunchy pecans and served with a hot toffee sauce which will help the ice cream to melt. Luscious layers of loveliness – get ready to tuck in.

FOR THE CAKE:

200 g/7 oz. shelled pecan halves

225 g/2 sticks butter, softened

225 g/generous 1 cup soft dark brown sugar

4 UK large/US extra-large eggs

190 g/1½ cups self-raising/self-rising flour

1 teaspoon baking powder

1 teaspoon ground cinnamon

1 teaspoon pure vanilla extract or ½ teaspoon vanilla bean powder

2 tablespoons natural/plain yogurt

FOR THE TOFFEE SAUCE:

100 g/½ cup soft dark brown sugar

100 g/7 tablespoons butter

300 ml/1¼ cups double/heavy cream

TO ASSEMBLE:

500 ml/2 cups praline and cream ice cream or vanilla ice cream

2 x 20-cm/8-inch round cake pans, greased and lined

SERVES 8

Preheat the oven to 180°C (350°F) Gas 4.

For the cake, in a food processor or blender, blitz 60 g/2 oz. of the pecans to very fine crumbs (the texture of ground almonds). In a mixing bowl, whisk together the softened butter and brown sugar until light and creamy. Add the eggs, one at a time, beating after each addition. Sift in the flour, baking powder, ground cinnamon and vanilla and fold in gently with the ground pecans and yogurt.

Spoon the batter into the prepared cake pans and arrange the remaining whole pecan halves in pretty patterns on top of the cakes. Bake in the preheated oven for 25–30 minutes until the cakes are golden brown and spring back to your touch and a knife comes out clean when inserted into the centre of one of the cakes. Turn the cakes out onto a wire rack to cool and remove the lining paper.

For the toffee sauce, heat the sugar and butter over a gentle heat in a saucepan until the sugar has dissolved. Add the cream and simmer for a few minutes until the sauce thickens slightly and you have a golden toffee-coloured sauce.

Brush a little of the toffee sauce over the top of the cakes to glaze, using a pastry brush. When you are ready to serve, place one of the cakes on a serving plate. Bring the ice cream to room temperature and place scoops of ice cream over the cake, spreading out in an even layer with a knife. Top with the second cake and then serve immediately with the remaining toffee sauce on the side, reheated if you wish.

Lemon meringue Arctic pie

I have fond childhood memories of the kitsch dessert, Arctic Roll. This is my rather grown-up version with pretty lemon layers, all wrapped up in a light citrus sponge. You can vary the flavours by using different ice creams or sorbets, jams, jellies or even chocolate spread.

FOR THE LEMON SPONGE:

4 UK large/US extra-large eggs

115 g/generous 1/2 cup caster/granulated sugar

grated zest of 1 lemon

115 g/3/4 cup plus 2 tablespoons self-raising/self-rising flour, sifted

1 teaspoon baking powder

FOR THE LEMON MERINGUE CREAM:

300 ml/13/4 cups double/heavy cream

2 heaped tablespoons lemon curd

2 meringue nests, crushed to small pieces

TO ASSEMBLE:

4 tablespoons lemon curd

300 ml/11/4 cups lemon sorbet or frozen lemon yogurt, slightly softened

icing/confectioners' sugar, for dusting

1 meringue nest, crushed to small pieces

34 x 30-cm/13 x 12-inch Swiss roll/jelly roll pan, greased and lined

20 x 12 x 9-cm/8 x 5 x 31/2-inch loaf pan, lined with a double layer of clingfilm/plastic wrap

SERVES 8

Preheat the oven to 180°C (350°F) Gas 4.

In a large mixing bowl, whisk together the eggs, caster/granulated sugar and lemon zest for about 5 minutes using an electric mixer until the mixture is very thick, creamy and pale. Sift together the flour and baking powder and fold very gently into the egg mixture with a spatula, trying not to knock out the air. Spoon the mixture into the Swiss roll/jelly roll pan and bake in the preheated oven for 15–20 minutes until golden brown and just firm to the touch. Turn the sponge out onto a sheet of baking parchment. Cover with a clean, damp kitchen towel and leave to cool.

Remove the towel and lining paper. Trim away the edges of the sponge using a sharp knife.

For the lemon meringue cream, whisk the double/heavy cream to stiff peaks then fold through the lemon curd and meringue pieces.

Cut out rectangles of sponge long enough to cover the base and wide sides of the loaf pan. Press into the pan to line. You need the sponge to come a little way above the top on each side. There is no need to put sponge on the short narrow sides.

Spoon half of the meringue cream mixture into the sponge case and spread out in an even layer. Spoon over two tablespoons of the lemon curd and spread into a thin layer. Cut the remaining sponge into two rectangles that are the size of the base of the loaf pan. Press one of the rectangles of cake into the loaf pan on top of the curd. Cover the sponge with the lemon sorbet and spread it out in an even layer. Cover with the remaining meringue cream and spread in an even layer. Depending on the depth of your pan, the layer may now be above the height of the pan. Do not worry as the whole cake will be wrapped in clingfilm/plastic wrap before freezing, which will hold it together. Spread over the remaining lemon curd and top with the second rectangle of sponge, pressing the overhanging sponge onto the sponge layer below. Tightly wrap the cake in clingfilm/plastic wrap and freeze for at least 3 hours.

When ready to serve, remove from the freezer and take off the outer clingfilm/plastic wrap. Use the lining clingfilm/plastic wrap to lift the cake from the pan. Invert the cake so that the joins are on the bottom and place on a serving plate. Bring to room temperature so that it is just soft enough to cut. Dust with icing/confectioners' sugar, sprinkle on the crushed meringue pieces and serve immediately. This cake will store in the freezer for up to 1 month.

Meringue and fruit sorbet layer cake

This colourful dessert is perfect for anyone who has a problem with dairy and/or gluten. It has pretty rainbow layers – I have used mango and raspberry sorbet but the flavour combination is entirely up to you. Lemon and lime work well, and strawberry and lemon is another winning combination. If you do not have time to make the sorbets yourself, it is fine to substitute store-bought sorbet for equally delicious results. It is important to use really ripe mangoes for the best flavour. You could even make mini individual meringue layers for each of your guests and allow them to pick from a choice of sorbet flavours and assemble their own towers.

4 UK large/US extra-large egg whites

225 g/generous 1 cup caster/granulated sugar

1 teaspoon pure vanilla extract or 1/2 teaspoon vanilla bean powder

FOR THE RASPBERRY SORBET:

340 g/3/4 lb. fresh raspberries

100 g/1/2 cup caster/granulated sugar

freshly squeezed juice of 1 lemon

FOR THE MANGO SORBET:

4 ripe mangos

200 g/1 cup caster/granulated sugar

TO ASSEMBLE:

icing/confectioners' sugar, for dusting

2 baking sheets, lined with silicon mats or non-stick baking parchment

ice cream machine

SERVES 8

Preheat the oven to 130°C (250°F) Gas 1/2.

In a mixing bowl, whisk the egg whites to stiff peaks. Add the caster/granulated sugar a spoonful at a time whisking so that you have a stiff, glossy meringue. Whisk in the vanilla.

Spread the meringue out into three round discs about 23 cm/ 9 inches in diameter on the baking sheets, with two discs on one sheet and one on the other sheet. Bake for 1–11/2 hours until the meringues are crisp and set and lightly golden coloured. If you are cooking the meringues on two shelves in the oven, the lower baking sheet may take longer to cook. Leave to cool on the baking sheets.

Place the raspberry sorbet ingredients with 250 ml/1 cup water in a saucepan and simmer for 10–15 minutes over a gentle heat until the sugar has dissolved and the raspberries are soft. Strain the mixture through a fine-mesh sieve/strainer to remove the raspberry seeds and leave to cool completely. Churn in an ice cream machine according to the manufacturer's instructions until the sorbet is frozen. If you do not have an ice cream machine, pour the raspberry mixture into a freezer-proof box and freeze until solid, whisking every 20 minutes or so to break up the ice crystals.

For the mango sorbet, peel and chop the mango flesh and blitz to a smooth paste in a blender, discarding the skins and seeds. Heat the sugar with 250 ml/1 cup water in a saucepan until the sugar has dissolved and you have a thin syrup. Cool the syrup then add to the blender with the mango purée and blitz again. Churn the purée in an ice cream machine following the manufacturer's instructions. If you do not have an ice cream machine, follow the instructions for freezing as set out above.

Store both sorbets in the freezer until you are ready to serve, then bring to room temperature until they are soft enough to scoop. Place one meringue on a serving plate, then place scoops of one of the sorbets on top. Gently cover with a second meringue, taking care as it is fragile. Place scoops of the other sorbet on top and then carefully top with the third meringue. Serve immediately.

Blackcurrant baked Alaska

Baked Alaska is one of those surprise-inside desserts which never fails to delight – hot toasted meringue with chilly blackcurrant ice cream makes this a perfect hot and cold dessert. It is important to only assemble at the last minute, as the hot meringue will start to melt the ice cream inside. If you want, you can make individual small Alaskas by cutting the cake into small circles and topping each with a scoop of ice cream, blackcurrants and a little meringue.

FOR THE CAKE:

115 g/generous 1/2 cup caster/granulated sugar

115 g/1 stick butter, softened

2 UK large/US extra-large eggs

115 g/3/4 cup plus 2 tablespoons self-raising/self-rising flour, sifted

1 teaspoon pure vanilla extract

115 g/4 oz. canned blackcurrants preserved in light syrup (drained weight, syrup reserved)

FOR THE MERINGUE:

150 g/3/4 cup caster/granulated sugar

60 ml/1/4 cup golden syrup/light corn syrup

125 ml/1/2 cup blackcurrant syrup (reserved from the canned blackcurrants)

3 UK large/US extra-large egg whites

1/2 teaspoon vanilla bean powder or 1 teaspoon pure vanilla extract

TO ASSEMBLE:

800 ml/scant 3 1/2 cups blackcurrant ripple ice cream

115 g/4 oz. canned blackcurrants preserved in light syrup (drained weight, syrup reserved)

20-cm/8-inch round cake pan, greased and lined

sugar thermometer

chef's blow torch

SERVES 8

Preheat the oven to 180°C (350°F) Gas 4.

To make the cake, in a large mixing bowl whisk together the caster/granulated sugar and butter until light and creamy. Add the eggs one at a time, whisking after each one is added. Gently fold in the self-raising/self-rising flour and vanilla. Fold in half of the drained blackcurrants. Spoon the cake batter into the prepared pan and sprinkle over the remaining blackcurrants. Bake in the preheated oven for 25–30 minutes until the cake is firm and springs back to your touch and a knife comes out clean when inserted into the centre of the cake. Turn the cake out onto a rack to cool completely.

For the meringue, simmer the sugar, golden syrup/light corn syrup and blackcurrant syrup until the sugar has dissolved, then bring to the boil. Using a sugar thermometer, heat the syrup to 119°C/238°F (soft-ball stage). In a clean dry bowl, whisk the egg whites to stiff peaks, then add the hot blackcurrant syrup in a small drizzle, whisking continuously together with the vanilla bean powder or pure vanilla extract. This is best done with a stand mixer, or if using a hand mixer, have someone else pour in the hot sugar syrup. Whisk for about 10 minutes then leave to cool.

When you are ready to serve, cut the cake in half horizontally and remove the lining paper. Place one of the cake halves on a serving plate. Spread a layer of the ice cream on top of the cake (the ice cream needs to be softened to room temperature) and sprinkle over half of the blackcurrants. Place the second cake on top and again pile high with another layer of ice cream and the remaining blackcurrants. Cover the whole cake and ice cream with the meringue, spreading it with a spatula into swirled patterns. It is important to make sure that the meringue is cooled before spreading over the ice cream. Toast the meringue with a blow torch and serve straight away.

Coconut and mango icebox terrine

Coconut and mango make a totally tropical combination and often appear together in Thai desserts. This is a delicate icebox dessert with pretty white and orange layers. The ice cream terrine is coated in a ginger crumb layer which adds a wonderful crunch.

FOR THE COCONUT ICE CREAM:

3 UK large/US extra-large egg yolks

100 g/1/2 cup caster/granulated sugar

400 ml/scant 1 3/4 cups full-fat coconut milk

200 ml/generous 3/4 cup double/ heavy cream

1 large ripe mango

FOR THE CRUMB LAYER:

200 g/7 oz. ginger biscuits/ cookies

100 g/7 tablespoons butter, melted and cooled

ice cream machine

24 x 10-cm/9 1/2 x 4-inch loaf pan

mandoline (optional)

SERVES 8

For the ice cream, in a mixing bowl, whisk together the egg yolks and caster/granulated sugar until very thick and creamy and doubled in size. Place the coconut milk and double/heavy cream in a saucepan and bring to the boil. Take off the heat and slowly pour the hot coconut mixture over the whisked egg yolks, whisking all the time. Return the coconut custard to the saucepan and heat until the custard starts to thicken. Remove from the heat and leave to cool completely.

Churn the cooled coconut custard in the ice cream machine following the manufacturer's instructions. Alternatively, if you do not have an ice cream machine, transfer to a freezer-proof container and place in the freezer, whisking every 20 minutes to break up the ice crystals until the ice cream is frozen. Place the loaf pan the freezer to chill.

Peel the mango and slice in very thin slices using a mandoline or a very sharp knife. Take care when cutting around the large seed.

Line the loaf pan with a double layer of clingfilm/plastic wrap and spread one-third of the ice cream over the base. Then place a layer of mango on top, using about half of the mango. Repeat with a second ice cream layer and more mango and then finish with the remaining ice cream. Wrap in more clingfilm/plastic wrap and freeze overnight.

To make the crumb layer, blitz the ginger biscuits/cookies to fine crumbs in a food processor or blender and then stir through the cooled melted butter. Place the buttery crumbs on a large plate. Remove the ice cream from the freezer and lift out of the loaf pan. Peel away the clingfilm/plastic wrap and then press the ice cream loaf into the crumbs so that it is coated all over in a thin layer of the crumbs. It is important to work quickly so that that ice cream does not melt. Re-line the pan with another double layer of clingfilm/ plastic wrap and return the crumb-coated ice cream to the pan and freeze for a further hour.

When you are ready to serve, remove the ice cream from the freezer, remove the clingfilm/plastic wrap and place on a serving plate. Bring to room temperature for a few minutes and then cut into slices to serve. This ice cream terrine will store for up to 1 month in the freezer.

celebration layers

The luscious layered desserts in this chapter are perfect to serve at special occasions such as birthdays, Easter, Christmas and Thanksgiving. Cute Stripy Spring Mousse Pots topped with sugared eggs are the ideal Easter treat, and the Chestnut Meringue Pie, Festive Gingerbread Bowl and Christmas Pudding Trifle are all great to serve around the holiday period. This chapter also contains a Spiced Rum Baumkuchen or 'Tree Cake', made by toasting batter spiked with rum, marzipan and cinnamon in thin layers to look like the rings inside a tree. All this is wrapped up in a luxurious chocolate and rum glaze.

Chocolate cheesecake tower

This cheesecake tower makes a spectacular centrepiece for a dessert table with two layers of delicious chocolate cheesecake covered in fresh berries. If you want to make a smaller version, halve the cheesecake ingredients and bake in a 23-cm/9-inch round pan for the same amount of time.

FOR THE BASE:

400 g/14 oz. digestive biscuits/ graham crackers

200 g/1¾ sticks butter

FOR THE FILLING:

200 g/7 oz. plain/semisweet chocolate (ideally 70% cocoa solids or more)

400 g/14 oz. cream cheese

250 g/9 oz. mascarpone cheese

250 ml/1 cup crème fraîche or sour cream

250 ml/1 cup double/heavy cream

6 UK large/US extra-large eggs

400-g/14-oz. can of condensed milk

150 g/1 cup white chocolate chips

TO ASSEMBLE:

mixture of fresh berries and physalis

icing/confectioners' sugar and unsweetened cocoa powder, for dusting

25-cm/10-inch round springform cake pan, greased and lined

18-cm/7-inch round springform cake pan, greased and lined

SERVES 14

Preheat the oven to 180°C (350°F) Gas 4.

Wrap the base and edges of the cake pans in clingfilm/plastic wrap to ensure that none of the cheesecake mixture leaks out while it is baking.

To make the base, blitz the digestive biscuits/graham crackers to fine crumbs in a food processor. Melt the butter in a saucepan and then stir into the crumbs, making sure that all the crumbs are coated. Divide the crumbs between the two cake pans, putting two-thirds into the large cake pan and one-third into the small cake pan. Press down flat with the back of a spoon.

For the filling, break the chocolate into pieces and place in a heatproof bowl resting over a pan of simmering water. Simmer until the chocolate has melted then leave to cool.

In a mixing bowl, whisk together the cream cheese, mascarpone, crème fraîche and cream until smooth. Add the eggs and condensed milk and whisk again. Whisk in the cooled melted chocolate until it is all incorporated and the cheesecake is an even colour. Stir in the white chocolate chips. Divide the mixture between the two cake pans, putting two-thirds into the large pan and one-third into the small pan.

Place the cake pans onto a baking sheet and transfer to the oven. Bake for 50–60 minutes until the cheesecakes are set but still have a slight wobble in the centre. Remove from the oven and leave to cool in their pans, then refrigerate until you are ready to serve.

To serve, remove the cheesecakes from the pans by sliding a knife around the edge and removing the pan bases and lining paper. Stack the smaller cheesecake on top of the larger one. Decorate with a mixture of fresh berries and physalis and dust with icing/ confectioners' sugar and cocoa powder. Serve immediately or store in the refrigerator until needed. The cheesecakes will store for up to 3 days in the refrigerator but are best decorated with the fruit just before serving.

Stripy spring mousse pots

These pretty, stripy mousse pots would make a lovely dessert, topped with sugar eggs, to serve after an Easter lunch. The raspberries give the mousse a beautiful pink colour without the need for any food colouring. For a special picnic, you can prepare them in small preserving jars so they are easy to transport.

FOR THE SPONGE:

115 g/1 stick butter, softened

115 g/generous ½ cup caster/granulated sugar

2 UK large/US extra-large eggs

60 g/scant ½ cup self-raising/self-rising flour, sifted

60 g/generous ½ cup ground almonds

FOR THE RASPBERRY LAYER:

150 g/5½ oz. raspberries

50 g/¼ cup caster/granulated sugar

300 ml/1¼ cups double/heavy cream

FOR THE LEMON LAYER:

freshly squeezed juice of 3 lemons

50 g/¼ cup caster/granulated sugar

300 ml/1¼ cups double/heavy cream

yellow food colouring gel or paste (optional)

TO DECORATE:

6 sugar-coated chocolate eggs

20-cm/8-inch round cake pan, greased and lined

6 glasses

2 piping/pastry bags, fitted with large round nozzles/tips

7-cm/3-inch round cutter (or just smaller than the size of your glasses)

MAKES 6

Preheat the oven to 180°C (350°F) Gas 4.

For the sponge, in a mixing bowl, whisk together the butter and caster/granulated sugar until very light and creamy. Beat in the eggs, one at a time, whisking after each egg is added. Gently fold in the flour and ground almonds. Spoon into the prepared cake pan and spread out into an even layer. Bake for about 20–25 minutes until the sponge is golden brown and springs back to your touch and a knife comes out clean when inserted into the centre. Leave to cool, then remove from the cake pan. Remove the lining paper.

Use the cutter to cut out six circles of the sponge. Depending on the actual size of your cutter and the size of the cake pan the sixth circle may be a slightly fluted shape, but this does not matter as it will be layered between the mousses.

For the raspberry layer, put a fine-mesh sieve/strainer over a bowl, place the raspberries inside and press down on them with the back of a spoon or a spatula to release all the juices. You should end up with just the seeds and a small amount of raspberry flesh in the sieve/strainer which you should discard. Add the sugar to the raspberry juice and stir for a few minutes until the sugar has dissolved. Pour in the double/heavy cream and whisk to soft peaks. Chill in the refrigerator while you make the lemon layer.

For the lemon layer, place the lemon juice and caster/granulated sugar in a bowl and stir until the sugar has dissolved. Pour in the cream and whisk to soft peaks, adding food colouring, if using.

Spoon the mousses into the two piping/pastry bags. Cut each disc of cake into quarters horizontally so that you have 24 discs of cake.

Pipe a large swirl of raspberry mousse into the glasses. Place a disc of cake on top of the cream in each glass. Next pipe a swirl of lemon mousse. Again top with a disc of cake. Repeat with layers of cake and mousse until the glasses are full. Chill in the refrigerator for at least 3 hours or overnight. Just before serving, decorate with the sugar eggs (do not do this sooner as the shells will dissolve). Store, covered, in the refrigerator for up to 3 days.

Chestnut meringue pie

This recipe is inspired by one of my favourite food love stories 'Food of Love', where a chef seeks to woo a girl by cooking her the most delicious food – it is my kind of book! In the book he makes a chestnut-stuffed meringue. I have never been able to find a recipe but have made my own with the marron paste below piped into soft meringue shells. They are yummy! This dessert is inspired by that story with pillowy meringue nestled over chestnut custard and a marron paste all wrapped up in a crunchy cookie case giving a delicious layer of loveliness.

FOR THE PIE CRUST:

300 g/10¹/₂ oz. Oreo cookies

125 g/9 tablespoons butter, melted

FOR THE MARRON PASTE:

100 g/3¹/₂ oz. unsweetened chestnut purée

100 g/3¹/₂ oz. pistachios, finely ground

2 tablespoons icing/confectioners' sugar, sifted

60 ml/¹/₄ cup double/heavy cream

FOR THE CUSTARD TOPPING:

5 UK large/US extra-large egg yolks

70 g/generous ¹/₄ cup caster/granulated sugar

375 ml/generous 1¹/₂ cups double/heavy cream

¹/₂ teaspoon vanilla bean powder or 1 teaspoon pure vanilla extract

300 g/10¹/₂ oz. unsweetened chestnut purée

FOR THE MERINGUE:

5 UK large/US extra-large egg whites

6 tablespoons caster/granulated sugar

25-cm/10-inch loose-bottomed tart pan, greased

SERVES 10

For the pie crust, place the Oreos in a food processor or blender and blitz to fine crumbs. Stir in the melted butter ensuring that all the crumbs are well coated. Press the crumbs into the base and sides of the tart pan.

Preheat the oven to 150°C (300°F) Gas 2.

For the marron paste, mix together the chestnut purée, ground pistachios, icing/confectioners' sugar and double/heavy cream. Spread out in a thin layer over the cookie crumb base.

For the custard, whisk together the egg yolks and sugar until thick and creamy. Slowly pour in the cream, whisking all the time. Whisk in the vanilla powder or pure vanilla extract and the chestnut purée. Carefully pour the custard over the marron paste. Bake in the oven for 1 hour until the custard layer has set but still has a slight wobble in the centre.

Just before the hour is up, prepare the meringue topping. Whisk the egg whites to stiff peaks. Add the sugar, a spoonful at a time, whisking all the time until the meringue is smooth and glossy. Remove the pie from the oven and, working very carefully and gently, spoon the meringue over the top of the chestnut custard and swirl into peaks. Take care as the custard will not be completely set. It is best to place small spoonfuls of meringue and then join them together by spreading gently with a palette knife. Bake in the preheated oven for 30–40 minutes until the meringue is golden brown and set. Remove from the oven and leave to cool completely. This pie will keep for up to 3 days stored in the refrigerator.

Ombre layer cake

This is a very simple cake, but it has the prettiest coloured effect when you cut into it. Each layer has a different flavour – chocolate, maple and cinnamon, coffee and vanilla – which all marry together perfectly to make one sumptuous mouthful. Wrapped in a whipped icing/frosting and decorated with pecans and chocolate curls, this is very easy to make, and would be lovely as a birthday cake for a special friend.

340 g/3 sticks butter, softened

340 g/1³/4 cups caster/granulated sugar

6 UK large/US extra-large eggs

340 g/2¹/2 cups self-raising/self-rising flour, sifted

3 tablespoons crème fraîche or sour cream

1 teaspoon pure vanilla extract

2 tablespoons unsweetened cocoa powder, sifted

2 tablespoons maple syrup

1 teaspoon ground cinnamon

orange food colouring gel or paste

1 teaspoon instant coffee granules

FOR THE ICING/FROSTING:

600 ml/2¹/2 cups double/heavy cream

100 g/³/4 cup icing/confectioners' sugar, sifted

¹/2 teaspoon vanilla bean powder or 1 teaspoon pure vanilla extract

FOR THE DECORATION:

200 g/7 oz. pecan halves

chocolate curls or sprinkles

4 x 20-cm/8-inch cake pans, greased and lined

piping/pastry bag fitted with a small round nozzle/tip

a serrated scraper, (optional)

SERVES 10

Preheat the oven to 180°C (350°F) Gas 4.

Whisk together the butter and caster/granulated sugar in a bowl using a mixer until light and creamy. Add the eggs one at a time and whisk again. Fold in the flour and crème fraîche using a spatula until everything is incorporated. Divide the cake batter into quarters in separate bowls. Add the vanilla extract to one bowl and fold in. Add the sifted cocoa powder to the second bowl and fold in. Add the maple syrup and ground cinnamon to the third bowl and fold in with a little orange food colouring. Dissolve the coffee in 2 tablespoons of hot water and then fold into the fourth mixture. Spoon the cake batters into the lined cake pans.

Bake the cakes for 25–30 minutes in the preheated oven. You may need to do this in two batches, cooking two cakes each time. Turn the cakes out onto wire racks and remove the lining paper. Leave the cakes to cool completely.

In a clean mixing bowl, whisk the double/heavy cream, icing/confectioners' sugar and vanilla to stiff peaks.

Place the chocolate cake on a cake plate or stand, securing it in place with a little cream underneath. Spread a layer of cream over the cake and then cover with the coffee cake. Repeat with another layer of cream and then top with the orange maple cake. Top with a little more cream and then top with the vanilla cake. Cover the top and sides of the cake in an even layer of the cream icing/frosting. For a decorative pattern, you can score lines in the cream using a serrated scraper. Place pecan halves around the top and base of the cake and decorate with a ring of chocolate curls on top.

Chill in the refrigerator until you are ready to serve. This cake will store in the refrigerator for up to 2 days, but is best eaten on the day it is made.

Spiced winter fruit zabaglione

Here a warm, foamy, wine-infused zabaglione is placed over ruby red fruits and slices of cinnamon sponge. Zabaglione does not keep, so you need to make it at the last minute and serve it straight away. The fruits are inspired by my friend chef Giancarlo Caldesi, who often serves roasted summer fruits baked with Cointreau – this is my winter version!

FOR THE FRUITS:

150 g/5^1/2 oz. blueberries

150 g/5^1/2 oz. blackberries

750 g/1 lb. 10 oz. red plums, halved and stones/pits removed

about 8 small clementines or satsumas, peeled

3 tablespoons caster/granulated sugar

1 teaspoon ground cinnamon

150 ml/^{2}/3 cup Cointreau or other orange liqueur

FOR THE CAKE:

115 g/1 stick butter, softened

115 g/generous ^{1}/2 cup caster/granulated sugar

2 UK large/US extra-large eggs

60 g/generous ^{1}/2 cup ground almonds

60 g/scant ^{1}/2 cup self-raising/self-rising flour

1 teaspoon baking powder

1 teaspoon ground cinnamon

1 teaspoon pure vanilla extract

125 ml/^{1}/2 cup dessert wine

FOR THE ZABAGLIONE:

100 g/^{1}/2 cup caster/granulated sugar

2 UK large/US extra-large eggs, plus 3 yolks

160 ml/scant ^{3}/4 cup dessert wine

20-cm/8-inch round cake pan, greased and lined

SERVES 8

Preheat the oven to 180°C (350°F) Gas 4.

For the fruits, place the blueberries, blackberries, plums and clementines in a large roasting pan. Sprinkle with the caster/granulated sugar and cinnamon and drizzle with the Cointreau. Bake for about 30 minutes until the plums are soft, then remove from the oven and leave to cool. Leave the oven on.

In a mixing bowl, whisk together the butter and caster/granulated sugar until light and creamy. Add the eggs, one at a time, whisking after each is added. Whisk in the ground almonds and sift in the flour, baking powder and ground cinnamon. Add the vanilla and fold everything in. Spoon into the prepared cake pan and bake in the preheated oven for 25–30 minutes until the cake is firm and springs back to your touch and a knife comes out clean when inserted into the centre of the cake. Turn out onto a wire rack, remove the lining paper and leave to cool.

When you are ready to assemble, cut the sponge into slices and use to line the base and lower sides of the glass dish. Pour the dessert wine over the sponge and then top with the roasted fruits and their cooking juices.

For the zabaglione, place 80 ml/5^1/2 tablespoons water in a large heatproof bowl resting over a saucepan of simmering water with the sugar, eggs and egg yolks and whisk over the heat for about 5 minutes until the egg mixture is very voluminous and foamy and holds a trail when you drag the beaters through it. Whisking all the time, slowly pour in the dessert wine in a thin drizzle. It is best to get someone to help you do this while you whisk. Whisk for a further 3–5 minutes.

Working quickly pour the warm zabaglione over the fruits and serve immediately. You can prepare the fruit base the day before, but as the zabaglione does not keep, you should only make this immediately before serving.

Festive gingerbread bowl

This is the perfect treat to serve in Autumn/Fall as it is filled with rich layers of pumpkin-spiced cream and golden custard. My recipe contains Armagnac-soaked gingerbread and treacle cookie crumbs, so omit the alcohol if serving to children. To decorate, use store-bought gingerbread men to give this dessert a playful feel.

FOR THE PUMPKIN CREAM:

300 g/10½ oz. pumpkin purée (such as Libby's)

½ teaspoon salt

2 teaspoons ground cinnamon

½ teaspoon vanilla bean powder or 1 teaspoon pure vanilla extract

1 teaspoon ground ginger

pinch of ground nutmeg

140 g/scant ¾ cup caster/granulated sugar

200 g/7 oz. crème fraîche or sour cream

280 g/10 oz. cream cheese

TO ASSEMBLE:

300 ml/1¼ cups double/heavy cream

200 g/7 oz. treacle or ginger biscuits/cookies

85 g/6 tablespoons butter, melted

300 g/10½ oz. ginger cake

80–100 ml/about ⅓ cup Armagnac

500 g/1 lb. 2 oz. ready-made custard

20 small gingerbread men

trifle dish

SERVES 10

Place the pumpkin purée, salt, cinnamon, vanilla, ginger, nutmeg and caster/granulated sugar in a saucepan and heat for a few minutes until the purée thickens and the sugar has dissolved. Set aside until cold.

Whisk together the cooled pumpkin purée, crème fraîche and cream cheese.

Whisk the double/heavy cream to stiff peaks. Place the treacle or ginger biscuits in a food processor or blender and blitz to fine crumbs. Stir in the melted butter so that all the crumbs are coated. Cut the ginger cake into about 18 thin slices.

Place a layer of ginger cake (about half the slices) over the base of a trifle dish and drizzle with half of the Armagnac. You can be more generous with the Armagnac if you want a really boozy dessert! Tuck some gingerbread men against the sides of the bowl.

Spoon over half of the pumpkin cream, then sprinkle with half of the buttery biscuit/cookie crumbs. Spoon over half of the custard and then top with the remaining ginger cake and drizzle with the rest of the Armagnac.

Press the remaining gingerbread men around the sides of the dish and then continue to layer up the bowl with the remaining pumpkin cream and then the custard. Top with the whipped cream and sprinkle with the remaining biscuit/cookie crumbs. Chill in the refrigerator for 3 hours or overnight before serving.

Sugar snow boozy brandy cream cake

This is a pretty layered cake dusted with icing/confectioners' sugar and piped with a boozy cream, and is a great cake to make for a wintery afternoon tea. The cake is flavoured with British Christmas pudding and mincemeat, ideal for using up Christmas leftovers. If you only have one or the other, simply double the quantity of the one you have. If you do not have either, replace with a grated apple and a handful of raisins or sultanas/golden raisins and add a little ground cinnamon for equally delicious results.

FOR THE CAKES:

300 g/2¾ sticks butter, softened

300 g/1½ cups caster/granulated sugar

1 teaspoon pure vanilla extract or ½ teaspoon vanilla bean powder

5 UK large/US extra-large eggs

1 teaspoon ground apple pie spice or ground cinnamon

2 tablespoons Christmas pudding

2 tablespoons mincemeat

60 ml/¼ cup natural/plain or Greek yogurt

300 g/2¼ cups self-raising/self-rising flour, sifted

FOR THE FILLING:

600 ml/2½ cups double/heavy cream

60 ml/¼ cup brandy

3 tablespoons icing/confectioners' sugar, sifted, plus extra for dusting

3 x 20-cm/8-inch round cake pans, greased and lined

piping/pastry bag, fitted with a large round nozzle/tip

SERVES 10

Preheat the oven to 180°C (350°F) Gas 4.

In a mixing bowl, whisk together the butter and caster/granulated sugar until light and creamy. Whisk in the vanilla and then add the eggs one at a time, whisking after each egg is added. Whisk in the apple pie spice or cinnamon, the Christmas pudding, mincemeat and yogurt. Sift in the flour and fold in gently. Divide the cake batter between the three prepared cake pans and bake in the preheated oven for 25–30 minutes until the cakes are golden brown and spring back to your touch, and a knife comes out clean when inserted into the centre of the cake. I can fit all three cake pans in my oven at the same time by arranging them in a triangle pattern, but if you cannot, then cook the cakes in batches.

Turn the cakes out onto a wire rack and leave to cool. Remove the lining paper.

In a large mixing bowl, whisk the double/heavy cream, brandy and icing/confectioners' sugar together until the cream forms stiff peaks. Spoon the cream into the piping/pastry bag.

Save the best-looking cake for the top and place one of the others on a serving plate or cake stand. Pipe the cream around the edge of the cake and then spread a thin layer of cream in the middle of the cream ring. If you want to make the cake extra boozy, you can drizzle each cake with a little brandy. Place the second cake on top and pipe another ring of cream and then fill the centre with cream in the same way. Repeat with the final layer.

Dust the cake very liberally with icing/confectioners' sugar and serve straight away or store in the refrigerator until needed. This cake is best eaten on the day it is made but will store for up to 2 days in the refrigerator.

Christmas tree meringue

For a festive party, why not make this spectacular Christmas tree. Although it looks complex it is actually very simple to prepare and the meringues can be made in advance. The meringue tree should be served with an amaretto cream on the side and berries or fruits.

FOR THE CAKE:

115 g/1 stick butter, softened

115 g/generous 1/2 cup caster/granulated sugar

2 UK large/US extra-large eggs

85 g/2/3 cup self-raising/self-rising flour

30 g/1/3 cup cocoa powder

2 tablespoons whole milk

FOR THE MERINGUE:

6 UK large/US extra-large egg whites

340 g/13/4 cups caster/granulated sugar

sugar sprinkles

FOR THE GANACHE:

50 g/2 oz. plain/semisweet chocolate, broken into pieces

15 g/1 tablespoon butter

1 tablespoon liquid glucose

100 ml/1/3 cup double/heavy cream

TO SERVE:

300 ml/11/4 cups double/heavy cream

60 ml/1/4 cup amaretto liqueur

20-cm/8-inch round cake pan, greased and lined

2–3 baking sheets, lined with silicon mats or baking parchment

large piping/pastry bag fitted with a large star nozzle/tip

MAKES 1 LARGE TREE

Preheat the oven to 180°C (350°F) Gas 4.

For the cake, cream together the butter and caster/granulated sugar until very light and creamy. Add the eggs, one at a time, whisking after each egg is added. Sift in the self-raising/self-rising flour and cocoa powder and fold in with the milk. Spoon into the prepared cake pan and bake in the preheated oven for 20–25 minutes until the cake is firm and springs back to your touch and a knife comes out clean when inserted into the centre of the cake. Leave on a wire rack to cool.

Reduce the oven temperature to 130°C (250°F) Gas 1/2.

For the meringues, in a large mixing bowl whisk the egg whites to very stiff peaks and then whisk in the caster/granulated sugar a spoonful at a time until you have a glossy meringue. Spoon the meringue into the piping/pastry bag. You may need to refill the piping/pastry bag with more of the meringue depending on the size of your piping/pastry bag.

For the tree you need to create about 10 rings of the meringue, each ring getting slightly smaller each time. To do this, I pipe circles of meringue around different sized plates and saucers but if you are using baking parchment you can draw the circles onto the underside of the paper and trace around each circle. Pipe a circle of meringue just around the edge of the plate, then carefully lift up the plate. I find it easiest to do this by sliding a sharp knife under the plate and applying pressure to the top of the plate, using the knife to prize it up. Do not worry too much if you touch the meringue ring with the plate, as you will pipe on top of it and this will not show. I start with a 20-cm/8-inch plate, get a little smaller each time and then, when the rings become small enough (at about 10 cm/4 inches), I pipe the circles free-hand. Pipe nine rings of meringue and then pipe a large star to top the tree.

Next pipe stars of meringue on top of each ring, pulling the piping/pastry bag away quickly each time so that the stars have points on them. Make sure that the points face to the outside of the ring, rather than inside, as you want them to be visible and form the branches of the tree. If you want to decorate the tree, sprinkle sugar sprinkles over the rings before baking (do not bake silver balls as these will melt during the baking process).

Once you have piped meringue stars around all of the rings, place the baking sheets in the preheated oven and bake for about 1-11/2 hours until the meringues are crisp. You are likely to need to bake the sheets in batches depending on the size of your oven.

Leave the meringues on the sheets to cool completely. When you lift the meringues off the baking sheets, handle them very carefully as they will be very fragile.

Next prepare the ganache. Heat the chocolate, butter, liquid glucose and double/heavy cream in a saucepan and simmer over a gentle heat until the chocolate and butter have melted. Leave the ganache to cool for a few minutes so that it thickens slightly.

With the cake on the wire rack, place a sheet of foil or baking parchment underneath to catch the drips and then pour the ganache over the cake, making sure that the top and sides of the cake are completely covered. Leave to set.

To present your tree, place the ganache-coated cake on a serving plate or cake stand and then carefully place the largest meringue ring on top. Stack all the other meringues on top, working from largest to smallest, ending with the single meringue star on top. The meringues themselves are loose so you will need to carry carefully to your table. If you prefer you can fix the meringues together with a little whipped cream, but I prefer the simple effect of having no cream.

For the cream to serve alongside, whisk the double/heavy cream with the amaretto and whisk to stiff peaks. Serve the whipped boozy cream on the side with the meringue. The cake is best eaten on the day it is made but the meringue rings will keep well for about 5 days stored in an airtight container, so can be prepared well ahead of any festive party.

Christmas pudding trifle

This recipe was inspired by Claire Dodd who appeared with me on 'Weekend Kitchen' on the BBC Three Counties Radio. Claire runs a catering company and one year she had a large Christmas dinner cancelled and was left with more Christmas pudding than she knew what to do with. So she created a Christmas pudding trifle! While it is made with leftovers, I would say that this dish is nice enough to serve as the main centrepiece for your Christmas lunch – combining the two Christmas classics: trifle and Christmas pudding. It is actually very light and has a delicious boozy kick. I've decorated the top with tiny sugar roses, but you could use holly sprigs (wrap the stalks in clingfilm/plastic wrap before inserting into the trifle).

115 g/1 stick butter, softened

115 g/generous 1/2 cup caster/granulated sugar

2 UK large/US extra-large eggs

115 g/3/4 cup plus 2 tablespoons self-raising/self-rising flour, sifted

1 teaspoon ground cinnamon

FOR THE DRIZZLE:

80 ml/5 1/2 tablespoons brandy

juice of 3 clementines

FOR THE PUDDING LAYER:

450 g/1 lb. ready-cooked Christmas pudding

60 ml/1/4 cup brandy

grated zest of 2 clementines and juice of 4 clementines

600 ml/2 1/2 cups ready-made custard

600 ml/2 1/2 cups double/heavy cream

sugar roses, to decorate

20-cm/8-inch round cake pan, greased and lined

large trifle dish

SERVES 8–10

Preheat the oven to 180°C (350°F) Gas 4.

In a mixing bowl, whisk together the butter and sugar until light and creamy. Add the eggs, one at a time, beating after each egg is added. Add 1 heaped tablespoon of the Christmas pudding and whisk in. Reserve the remainder of the pudding for the Christmas pudding layer below. Fold in the flour and ground cinnamon. Spoon into the prepared cake pan and bake in the preheated oven for 25–30 minutes until the cake is golden brown and springs back to your touch and a knife comes out clean when inserted into the centre of the cake.

Turn the cake out onto a wire rack, remove the lining paper and cool completely. Cut the cooled cake into slices and place in an even layer over the base of the trifle dish. Whisk together the drizzle ingredients and pour over the sponge to soak it.

Place the reserved Christmas pudding, 60 ml/1/4 cup brandy, the clementine zest and juice in a blender and blitz until smooth. Pour the Christmas pudding mixture over the cake, then spread over the custard.

In a clean mixing bowl, whisk the double/heavy cream to soft peaks and spoon over the custard. Chill in the refrigerator for at least 3 hours. Just before serving, decorate with sugar roses if you wish. The trifle will keep for up to 3 days in the refrigerator.

Spiced rum baumkuchen

Baumkuchen is a cake of German origin, popular at Christmas time. It is also known as 'Tree Cake' due to the rings that are visible in the cake when you cut into it. Traditionally, baumkuchen is made on a spit over a fire, which creates the classic rings and hole in the middle. Obviously cooking on a spit at home is not very practical, so my version is made under the grill/broiler in a ring pan. It tastes just as fabulous.

FOR THE CAKE BATTER:

200 g/1¾ sticks butter, softened

150 g/¾ cup caster/granulated sugar

150 g/5½ oz. golden marzipan, cut into small pieces

8 eggs, separated

250 ml/1 cup double/heavy cream

60 ml/¼ cup rum

1 teaspoon ground cinnamon

½ teaspoon vanilla bean powder or 1 teaspoon pure vanilla extract

pinch of salt

140 g/1 cup self-raising/self-rising flour

100 g/1 cup cornflour/cornstarch

FOR THE GLAZE:

100 g/3½ oz. plain/semisweet chocolate, broken into pieces

1 tablespoon golden syrup or light corn syrup

150 ml/⅔ cup double/heavy cream

60 ml/¼ cup rum

15 g/1 tablespoon butter

TO DECORATE:

50 g/2 oz. white chocolate, melted

25-cm/10-inch round flat-bottomed ring pan, such as an Angel cake pan

SERVES 10

Cream together the butter and sugar until light and creamy. Add the chopped marzipan and whisk into the butter mixture. Add the egg yolks and whisk in. Add the double/heavy cream, rum, ground cinnamon, vanilla and salt and whisk to make a smooth batter.

Sift in the self-raising/self-rising flour and cornflour/cornstarch and fold in until incorporated.

In a separate bowl, whisk the egg whites to stiff peaks and then fold into the batter by first taking a large spoonful of egg white and beating it in to loosen, and then folding in the rest gently a spoonful at a time, trying not to knock out all of the air.

Place about two large spoonfuls of batter into the pan and spread out with a silicon pastry brush or a spatula into a very thin layer. You should not be able to see the base of the pan through the batter.

Bake under a hot grill/broiler for about 3–5 minutes until the top of the batter turns golden brown. The cooking time will depend on many factors such as how hot the grill is and how far your pan is from the grill, so watch carefully. Once the first layer is done you will have a good idea on timings for the rest. When the top is golden brown, carefully remove from the grill/broiler and place another two spoonfuls of batter on top. Spread them out in the same way as before, making sure that all of the cake below is covered but keeping the layers thin. Cook again in the same way and continue until the batter is used up. It should make about 10 layers, although this depends on the size of pan and thickness of the batter. As the number of layers increases the top of the cake will be nearer to the grill and therefore will cook faster, so watch very carefully towards the end. Once finished, slide a knife around the edge of the pan to prevent sticking and leave the cake in the pan to cool.

Remove the cooled cake from the pan and invert onto a cooling rack, placing foil or baking parchment underneath to catch drips.

In a saucepan heat the chocolate, syrup, cream, rum and butter until melted together into a smooth glossy sauce. Pour the glaze over the top and sides of the cake and leave to set. Drizzle with thin lines of melted white chocolate to decorate and leave to set.

This cake will store for up to 3 days in an airtight container or longer if stored in the refrigerator.

round the world layers

Sweet treats from around the Globe are featured in this chapter. The American PieCaken, a pie baked between layers of sponge and white chocolate blondie, is the ultimate kitsch layer cake. There is flaky layered filo pastry Baklava from Greece, classic Opera Cake from France and Hungarian Strawberry Pastry Bars. Last but not least, a beautiful domed Swedish Princess Cake, fit for royalty. It is a delicious cake with layers of sponge, raspberry jam and sweetened cream, covered with a thin layer of green marzipan and finished with a marzipan rose.

American Piecaken

A 'Piecaken' is a quirky American classic right up there with the 'Turducken'. It is one of the most kitsch foods I know, as you take a store-bought pie and bake it between layers of cinnamon sponge and white chocolate blondie. This is the ultimate layer cake! Served warm, this makes a mouthwatering dessert with custard.

FOR THE BLONDIE LAYER:

100 g/3½ oz. white chocolate, broken into pieces

125 g/9 tablespoons butter

3 UK large/US extra-large eggs

200 g/1 cup caster/granulated sugar

1 teaspoon pure vanilla extract

pinch of vanilla salt or regular salt

120 g/1 cup plain/all-purpose flour

FOR THE SPONGE CAKE:

115 g/1 stick butter, softened

115 g/generous ½ cup soft dark brown sugar

2 UK large/US extra-large eggs

115 g/¾ cup plus 2 tablespoons self-raising/self-rising flour, sifted

1 teaspoon ground cinnamon

60 ml/¼ cup milk

FOR THE PIE LAYER:

1 store-bought apple pie, about 18 cm/7 inches in diameter

FOR THE FROSTING GLAZE:

200 g/1½ cups icing/confectioners' sugar, sifted

30 ml/2 tablespoons apple schnapps or apple juice

2 tablespoons salted caramel sauce or toffee sauce

15 g/1 tablespoon butter

23-cm/9-inch round springform cake pan, greased and lined

SERVES 10

Preheat the oven to 180°C (350°F) Gas 4.

Begin by preparing the blondie layer. Place the white chocolate pieces and butter in a heatproof bowl resting over a saucepan of simmering water and stir until both the butter and chocolate have melted. Take care that no water gets into the bowl. Leave to cool slightly.

Whisk together the eggs and caster/granulated sugar using an electric whisk until the mixture is thick and creamy and has doubled in size. Add the chocolate mixture and whisk in. Add the vanilla extract, vanilla salt (or regular salt) and flour and fold in gently. Pour the mixture into the prepared cake pan. Bake for 20 minutes in the preheated oven until the top of the blondie has formed a crust.

While the blondie is cooking, prepare the sponge cake. In a mixing bowl, whisk together the butter and dark brown sugar until light and creamy. Add the eggs, one at a time, whisking after each one is added. Fold in the flour and ground cinnamon gently. Add the milk to loosen the batter.

When the blondie layer has baked for 20 minutes, remove the cake pan from the oven, leaving the oven on and carefully place the apple pie on top. Do not press down as you want it to rest on top of the blondie layer. Carefully spoon over the cinnamon sponge, making sure that all of the pie is covered and return to the oven to bake for a further 25–35 minutes until the sponge springs back to your touch. Remove from the oven and leave to cool in the pan.

For the frosting glaze, place the icing/confectioners' sugar in a saucepan with the apple schnapps or apple juice, the caramel sauce and butter and heat until you have a smooth frosting. Pass through a fine-mesh sieve/strainer to remove any lumps of icing/confectioners' sugar. Remove the sides and base of the cake pan and place on a cooling rack with a sheet of foil or baking parchment underneath to catch any drips. Pour over the warm frosting and leave to set, then transfer to a cake plate to serve. This cake will store for up to 3 days in an airtight container but is best eaten on the day it is made.

Italian Gianduja cake

This recipe is inspired by the wonderful Italian Gianduja chocolates, made with chocolate and hazelnuts. An indulgent block of Gianduja chocolate fills the middle of this yummy cake.

FOR THE GIANDUJA:

100 g/3$\frac{1}{2}$ oz. milk chocolate pieces

50 g/2 oz. plain/semisweet chocolate pieces

130 g/4$\frac{1}{2}$ oz. skinned roasted hazelnuts

100 g/$\frac{3}{4}$ cup icing/confectioners' sugar, sifted

2–3 teaspoons unflavoured oil

FOR THE SPONGE:

4 UK large/US extra-large eggs

115 g/generous $\frac{1}{2}$ cup caster/granulated sugar

50 g/6 tablespoons self-raising/self-rising flour, sifted

50 g/2 oz. ground roasted hazelnuts

FOR THE HAZELNUT CREAM:

300 ml/1$\frac{1}{4}$ cups double/heavy cream

100 g/3$\frac{1}{2}$ oz. plain/semisweet chocolate, melted and cooled

1 heaped tablespoon hazelnut-chocolate spread

TO DECORATE:

100 g/3$\frac{1}{2}$ oz. plain/semisweet chocolate, broken into pieces

1 tablespoon liquid glucose (or golden syrup/light corn syrup)

150 ml/$\frac{2}{3}$ cup double/heavy cream

30 g/2 tablespoons butter

chopped roasted hazelnuts

2 x 25 x 12-cm/10 x 5-inch loaf pans, double-lined with clingfilm/plastic wrap

35 x 25-cm/14 x 10-inch cake pan, greased and lined with baking parchment

SERVES 8–10

For the Gianduja, put all the chocolate in a heatproof bowl set over a pan of simmering water and heat until melted. Put 100 g/3$\frac{1}{2}$ oz. of the hazelnuts in a food processor with half the icing/confectioners' sugar and all the oil. Blitz to a smooth paste, then add to the melted chocolate with the remaining sugar. Beat to a smooth paste with a spatula.

Spoon half the paste into one of the prepared loaf pans, spread in an even layer, sprinkle the remaining whole hazelnuts over the Gianduja, then cover with the rest of the paste. Chill in the refrigerator until set firm. Remove from the pan and store in the refrigerator, still wrapped.

Preheat the oven to 180°C (350°F) Gas 4.

For the sponge, whisk together the eggs and caster/granulated sugar until very thick, creamy and tripled in size. Gently fold in the flour and ground hazelnuts. Spoon into the prepared pan and carefully spread in an even layer. Bake in the preheated oven for 12–14 minutes until golden brown on top and springy to your touch. Turn the cake out and remove the lining paper. Leave to cool.

For the hazelnut cream, whisk together the cream, melted and cooled chocolate and hazelnut-chocolate spread to stiff peaks. It is important that the chocolate is cooled as if not, it will solidify in strands in the cream.

Cut half of the cake into pieces large enough to cover the base and longer sides of the second loaf pan and press into the prepared pan. Spoon half the hazelnut cream into the cake case. Cut the remaining cake into three rectangles, cutting one of them in half. Lay one of the small rectangles and one of the large rectangles side by side in a layer to give a piece of cake the length of the loaf pan so the hazelnut cream is covered.

Unwrap the Gianduja and spread a thin layer of cream over the previous cake layer, then place the Gianduja block on top and cover with the remaining hazelnut cream. Cover with the remaining cake and press the top sides of the cake down. Use any excess lining from the loaf pan to wrap the whole cake tightly in clingfilm/plastic wrap and refrigerate for at least 3 hours.

To decorate, heat the chocolate, liquid glucose, cream and butter in a pan to make a smooth glossy sauce. Unwrap the cake and set on a cooling rack with a sheet of baking parchment beneath, then pour the sauce all over the cake. Sprinkle with chopped hazelnuts. Refrigerate again for 1 hour until set. Serve or store for up to 2 days in the refrigerator.

Opera cake

Opera cake is a luxurious multi-layered slice, here flavoured with a delicious coffee buttercream, rich chocolate ganache and a light joconde sponge. Joconde sponge is made using whisked eggs and billowing meringue, which makes the lightest sponge. It is then soaked in a boozy coffee syrup. It is important that the cakes and syrup are cool before you assemble the cake. I am not going to fib, this cake takes time and patience, but it is worth the effort for a special occasion. You can also prepare the buttercream and syrup ahead of time to make the process less complex.

For the buttercream, heat the caster/granulated sugar and espresso coffee in a saucepan over a gentle heat until the sugar has dissolved, then bring to the boil and boil until the temperature reaches soft ball stage – this is 119°C/238°F on a sugar thermometer, or when you drop a little of the caramel into a glass of cold water it will form a ball which is soft.

While the caramel is cooking, whisk the egg yolks in a separate bowl until light and creamy. Turn the speed down and slowly pour in the coffee caramel. Whisk until the mixture is light and voluminous and has cooled completely. Slowly add in the butter, a spoonful at a time, whisking all the time until the butter is all incorporated. Whisk for a few minutes more until the mixture is light and airy. Chill in the refrigerator while you prepare the cake.

Preheat the oven to 200°C (400°F) Gas 6.

For the joconde sponge, separate four of the eggs. Place the four yolks in a heatproof bowl resting over a pan of simmering water with the four whole eggs and the icing/confectioners' sugar. Whisk over the heat for about 3–5 minutes. Remove from the heat and whisk the eggs for a few minutes more with an electric mixer until doubled in size.

In a separate clean bowl, whisk the egg whites to stiff peaks. Slowly add the caster/granulated sugar a spoonful at a time to make a meringue.

Fold the ground almonds and flour into the egg yolk mixture, then slowly fold in the meringue one-third at a time until it is all incorporated. Divide the mixture between the two cake pans and spread out thinly. Bake the cakes for 10–14 minutes in the preheated oven until lightly golden brown. Remove from the oven and turn out onto sheets of baking parchment and carefully remove the lining paper. Before inverting the pans, slide a sharp knife along the edge of the cake to release it. Leave the cakes to cool.

For the coffee syrup, in a saucepan heat the coffee and caster/granulated sugar. Add the instant coffee and dissolve. Bring the mixture to the boil and simmer for a few minutes until syrupy. Remove from the heat and leave to cool then add the coffee liqueur.

For the ganache, in a saucepan heat the cream, butter, chocolate and liquid glucose and simmer until the chocolate and butter have melted and you have a smooth glossy sauce.

Cut the cakes in half so that you have four rectangles of cake in total. Place one rectangle on the cake board. Carefully drizzle over some of the coffee syrup so that the sponge is soaked well in a thin layer of syrup. Carefully spread over a layer of the buttercream. Place a second sponge on top, soak with the coffee syrup and cover with a thin layer of the ganache. Place the third sponge on top and drizzle over more coffee syrup. Cover with another layer of buttercream. Place the final sponge on top but this time do not cover with coffee syrup.

Cover the top of the cake with the ganache. Do not worry if it runs down the sides of the cake a little as you will trim the cake before serving.

FOR THE BUTTERCREAM:

225 g/generous 1 cup caster/
granulated sugar

60 ml/¹/₄ cup espresso coffee

4 UK large/US extra-large egg
yolks

300 g/2³/₄ sticks butter

FOR THE JOCONDE SPONGE:

8 UK large/US extra-large eggs

100 g/³/₄ cup icing/confectioners'
sugar, sifted

100 g/¹/₂ cup caster/granulated
sugar

200 g/7 oz. ground almonds

60 g/scant ¹/₂ cup self-raising/
self-rising flour, sifted

FOR THE COFFEE SYRUP:

120 ml/¹/₂ cup espresso coffee

100 g/¹/₂ cup caster/granulated
sugar

2 teaspoons instant coffee
granules

2 tablespoons coffee liqueur

FOR THE CHOCOLATE
GANACHE:

250 ml/1 cup double/heavy cream

30 g/2 tablespoons butter

100 g/3¹/₂ oz. plain/semisweet
chocolate, broken into pieces

2 tablespoons liquid glucose (or
golden syrup/light corn syrup)

TO DECORATE:

30 g/1 oz. white chocolate,
melted

finely chopped pistachios

edible gold leaf

sugar thermometer

*2 large rectangular baking pans,
greased and lined*

piping/pastry bag

SERVES 12

Place the melted white
chocolate into a piping/pastry
bag and pipe a design of your
choice – I've opted for treble
clefs but some like to write the
word 'Opera' on top of the cake
in pretty writing together with
some decorative patterns. For
extra decoration, sprinkle with
pistachios or use a little gold
leaf to make the cake look extra
special. Chill in the refrigerator.

When you are ready to serve,
trim away the sides of the
cake to make them neat and to
reveal the layers. The cake will
store for up to 3 days in the
refrigerator.

Smith Island cake

This is a beautiful multi-layered cake which stems from Smith Island in Maryland, USA. It comprises layers of vanilla sponge sandwiched together with a rich chocolate milk frosting. You can decorate the top with pretty sugar flowers or with chocolate curls or ribbons. As it has so many layers you only need to serve thin slices. There is some debate about how many layers this cake should have – mine has 10, which is plenty, but you can add more layers if you wish!

FOR THE SPONGE CAKE:

340 g/3 sticks butter, softened

340 g/1³/₄ cups caster/granulated sugar

6 UK large/US extra-large eggs

340 g/2¹/₂ cups self-raising/self-rising flour, sifted

1 teaspoon vanilla bean powder or 2 teaspoons pure vanilla extract

250 ml/1 cup low-fat natural/plain yogurt

FOR THE FROSTING:

225 g/generous 1 cup caster/granulated sugar

180 ml/³/₄ cup evaporated milk

100 ml/¹/₃ cup condensed milk

125 g/generous ³/₄ cup icing/confectioners' sugar

200 g/7 oz. plain/semisweet chocolate (ideally 70% cocoa solids), chopped

125 g/9 tablespoons butter

sugar flowers, to decorate

5 x 20-cm/8-inch round cake pans, greased and lined

SERVES 10

Preheat the oven to 180°C (350°F) Gas 4.

For the sponge cake, whisk together the butter and sugar until light and creamy. Whisk in the eggs one at a time. Fold in the flour, vanilla and yogurt gently until everything is incorporated. Divide the mixture between the five lined cake pans, spreading the mixture out evenly. Bake the cakes for about 20–25 minutes in the preheated oven until the cakes spring back to your touch. If you do not have enough pans, then cook the mixture in batches, washing the pans and relining them between each use. Leave the cakes in the pans for a few minutes to cool, then turn out onto a rack to cool completely. Cut each cake in half horizontally once cooled using a serrated knife.

For the frosting, heat the caster/granulated sugar in a saucepan with the evaporated and condensed milks until the sugar has dissolved. Add the icing/confectioners' sugar, chocolate and butter and heat gently, whisking all the time, until the butter and chocolate have melted. Pass the frosting through a fine-mesh sieve/strainer to remove any lumps. Leave to cool for a while so that the frosting starts to thicken.

Place one of the cakes on a cake stand with sheets of foil or baking parchment tucked under the sides of the cake – this is to prevent the frosting from covering the cake stand. Place two large spoons of frosting over the cake and spread out in a thin layer so that all of the cake is covered. Place the next cake on top. It is best to place the cakes with the non-cut side face up so that the frosting does not sink into the soft middle of the cake. Do not worry if any of the cakes break, as this will not be visible when sliced. Repeat with the remaining layers so that each is sandwiched with some of the chocolate fudge icing.

Spread the remaining frosting over the top and the sides of the cake and leave to set. Reserve a little of the frosting for attaching the sugar flowers. When the frosting has set into a glossy layer, affix the sugar flowers using the reserved frosting and carefully remove the foil so that the cake is neat on your cake plate. This cake will store for up to 3 days wrapped in clingfilm/plastic wrap or in an airtight container, but, as with all cakes, it is best eaten on the day it is made.

Pineapple and coconut millefeuilles

Classic millefeuilles are always a treat and this Caribbean-inspired version is truly delicious, featuring crisp glazed pastry filled with coconut rum cream, pineapple compote and caramelized pineapple slices. Although you can make your own puff pastry, it does take time and so using store-bought puff pastry is completely acceptable!

500 g/1 lb. 2 oz. all-butter puff pastry

1 UK large/US extra-large egg, beaten

plain/all-purpose flour, for dusting

caster/granulated sugar, for dusting

FOR THE PINEAPPLE COMPOTE AND GRIDDLED PINEAPPLE:

1 large ripe pineapple, peeled and eyes removed

60 ml/¼ cup coconut rum

60 g/5 tablespoons caster/granulated sugar, plus extra for sprinkling

FOR THE COCONUT CREAM:

450 ml/generous 1¾ cups double/heavy cream

70 ml/generous ¼ cup coconut rum

1 tablespoon icing/confectioners' sugar, sifted, plus extra for dusting

3 large baking sheets, lined with baking parchment

piping/pastry bag fitted with a large star nozzle/tip

MAKES 6

Preheat the oven to 200°C (400°F) Gas 6.

On a flour-dusted surface, roll out the pastry to a 36-cm/14-inch square. Brush the top with a little beaten egg and sprinkle with a little caster/granulated sugar. Cut into three long equal strips.

Place one of the pastry strips on one of the lined baking sheets and cover with baking parchment. Place a second lined baking sheet on top and place the two remaining pastry slices on top. Again cover with baking parchment and place the third baking sheet on top. (If you do not have 3 baking sheets you can cook the pastry in batches. However, placing the sheets on top prevents the pastry from rising too much and losing its shape.)

Bake for 40–50 minutes in the preheated oven until the pastry is golden brown and cooked all the way through. Leave to cool.

Thinly slice half of the pineapple into 12 slices. Core the remaining pineapple and chop the flesh into small pieces. Place the flesh in a saucepan with the 60 ml/¼ cup coconut rum, 60 ml/¼ cup water and the sugar and simmer for about 10 minutes until soft. Blitz to a smooth purée in a blender then set aside to cool.

Heat a griddle pan until very hot and sprinkle the pineapple slices with a little caster/granulated sugar on both sides. Place in the pan and griddle for about 5 minutes on each side or until caramelized. Remove from the heat and leave to cool. The cooking time depends on the heat of the griddle and ripeness of the fruit.

For the coconut cream, place the double/heavy cream and coconut rum in a mixing bowl with the icing/confectioners' sugar and whisk to stiff peaks. Spoon into the piping/pastry bag.

When you are ready to assemble, trim the edges of the pastry and cut each slice into six equal rectangles. Pipe small stars of cream around the edge of two-thirds of the pastry slices, leaving a gap in the middle. Fill the gaps with a teaspoon of the pineapple purée. Assemble the pastry stacks by placing two cream-topped slices on top of each other, each time topping the cream with a griddled slice of pineapple. Top with a plain pastry slice and dust with icing/confectioners' sugar. Repeat with the remaining slices. Serve straight away or store in the refrigerator until needed. These are best eaten on the day they are made.

Cranberry and pecan baklava

Baklava is one of the most popular desserts in Greece – it amazes me how crisp the bakeries can get the pastry, soaked in a sweet honey syrup. Baklava is great to serve alongside coffee for a morning treat or afternoon pick-me-up. While traditionally made with walnuts, this is my cranberry and pecan version. The fruit adds a delicious flavour and texture, but if you want to be a purist, you can replace the pecans with walnuts and omit the cranberries.

FOR THE FRUIT AND NUT FILLING:

200 g/7 oz. pecans

75 g/2½ oz. dried cranberries

100 g/½ cup caster/granulated sugar

2 teaspoons ground cinnamon

½ teaspoon vanilla bean powder or 1 teaspoon pure vanilla extract

225 g/8 oz. filo/phyllo pastry

150 g/1¼ sticks butter, melted

FOR THE SYRUP:

160 ml/scant ¾ cup runny honey

freshly squeezed juice of 1 small orange

25-cm/10-inch square loose-bottomed cake pan, greased

MAKES 25 SQUARES

Preheat the oven to 200°C (400°F) Gas 6.

Place the pecans, dried cranberries, caster/granulated sugar, ground cinnamon and vanilla bean powder or vanilla extract in a food processor or blender and blitz to fine crumbs.

When working with filo/phyllo pastry you have to be careful as it can quickly dry out in the heat of your kitchen, so keep it covered with a damp clean kitchen towel while you work. Filo/phyllo pastry comes in large sheets but the sizes of the sheets can vary so you will need to cut the sheets to fit the size of the cake pan. The sheets I usually buy are large enough to cut into two-third-and one-third-pieces, with the larger square large enough to cover the base of the whole cake pan and then two of the smaller rectangles being used to make an alternating layer of the same size. Once baked the divides in some of the layers will not be visible.

Place one of the larger sheets in the base of the cake pan and brush generously with the melted butter, using a pastry brush. Repeat with another 2–3 layers and then sprinkle over a handful of the nut mixture in a thin layer so that all the pastry is covered in a thin layer of nuts. Cover with one of the pastry squares, repeat the butter brushing and add another 2–3 layers of pastry. Add another layer of nuts and continue to layer up until all the pastry is used up and making sure that you end with a pastry layer on top. You may not need all of the nut mixture, but this can be saved in a jar or folded into a cake batter to make a delicious cake.

Brush the top of the baklava with plenty of butter and bake in the preheated oven for 15 minutes, then turn the temperature down to 180°C (350°F) Gas 4 and bake for a further 25–30 minutes until the pastry is crisp and golden brown. Remove from the oven. Heat the honey with the orange juice in a saucepan and then spoon over the top of the baklava. Leave the syrup to soak into the baklava while it cools, then cut into 25 squares to serve. The baklava will keep well for 3 days in an airtight container.

Hungarian strawberry pastry bars

This classic Hungarian layer pastry has tempting layers of strawberry jam/jelly and pistachios, all topped with a chocolate glaze – think strawberry Danish meets chocolate éclair. You can swap the pistachios and jam/jelly for any other nuts or flavours you prefer.

FOR THE PASTRY:

7 g/¼ oz. packet fast-action dried yeast

4 tablespoons caster/granulated sugar

200 ml/generous ¾ cup warm milk

600 g/4½ cups plain/all-purpose flour, sifted

180 g/1½ sticks butter, softened

2 UK large/US extra-large eggs, plus 1 yolk

grated zest of 1 lemon

1 teaspoon pure vanilla extract

2 tablespoons crème fraiche or sour cream

FOR THE FILLING:

150 g/5½ oz. shelled pistachios, blitzed in a food processor or blender until fine

1 jar of good quality strawberry jam/jelly (approx. 370 g/13 oz.)

FOR THE CHOCOLATE GLAZE:

100 g/3½ oz. plain/semisweet chocolate, broken into pieces

15 g/1 tablespoon butter

1 tablespoon liquid glucose (or golden syrup/light corn syrup)

100 ml/⅓ cup double/heavy cream

35 x 25-cm/14 x 10-inch large baking pan, greased and lined

MAKES 24

Place the yeast, sugar and warm milk in a jug/pitcher, stir and leave in a warm place for about 10 minutes until a foam has formed on top of the milk. It is important that you use only warm milk and not hot milk, otherwise it may kill the yeast.

Place the flour, butter, eggs, yolk, lemon zest, vanilla and crème fraîche into the bowl of a stand mixer and mix with a dough hook. Alternatively rub the mixture together with your hands. Once the foam has formed on the milk, add to the flour mixture and knead with a dough hook or by hand for about 5–8 minutes until very soft and pliable but not too sticky. Add a little flour if needed.

Cover the bowl with a damp kitchen towel and leave the dough in a warm place for an hour or until the dough has doubled in size.

Tip the dough onto a flour-dusted surface and knock it back with your hands to remove some of the air. The dough should feel soft and pliable and should move as you touch it – almost as if it is alive. Cut the dough into three equal portions. Using a rolling pin and dusting liberally with flour on a clean work surface, roll out one-third of the dough into a rectangle the size of your baking pan. Place the dough into the base of the pan, using the rolling pin to help you lift it and press out with your fingertips to cover the base of the baking pan.

Spread about half of the jam/jelly over the pastry layer in the pan, almost to the edges. If your jam/jelly is hard, mix with a spoon first so it is easy to spread. Sprinkle over half the ground pistachios.

Roll out a second third of the dough in the same way and cover the pistachio layer with the dough. Press out in the same way so that the jam/jelly and pistachios are completely covered. Spread over the remaining jam/jelly and sprinkle with the remaining pistachios, then cover with a third layer of rolled-out dough.

Preheat the oven to 180°C (350°F) Gas 4.

Cover the baking pan with a damp kitchen towel and leave to rise for 30 minutes. Once risen, bake for 30–40 minutes until golden brown.

For the chocolate glaze, heat the chocolate and butter in a saucepan with the liquid glucose and cream until melted into a smooth glossy sauce. Let cool slightly, then spoon over the top of the slice. Leave to cool in the saucepan. Lift the slice from the pan and remove the lining paper. Trim the edges of the pastry to neaten. Cut into 24 slices to serve. These slices are best eaten on the day they are made but can be stored for up to 2 days in an airtight container.

Kalter hund

This is a popular German layer cake made with a rich, boozy chocolate ganache and 'butterkeks' or butter biscuits/cookies. 'Kalter hund' actually translates as 'cold dog', which I have to admit does not sound appealing but I can assure you it is worth trying! In the UK you can also use Rich Tea finger biscuits. This is a great chocolate slice to make ahead and keep in the refrigerator as it stores well.

250 g/2¼ sticks butter

100 g/3½ oz. plain/semisweet chocolate (70% cocoa solids)

3 UK large/US extra-large eggs

75 ml/5 tablespoons amaretto liqueur

160 g/generous 1 cup icing/confectioners' sugar, sifted

80 g/generous ¾ cup unsweetened cocoa powder, sifted

250 g/9 oz. butter biscuits/cookies or Rich Tea finger biscuits

100 g/3½ oz. white chocolate

23 x 10 x 6-cm/9 x 4 x 2½-inch loaf pan

SERVES 10

Begin by preparing the loaf pan. Line it with a triple layer of clingfilm/plastic wrap as you will need a thick layer to be able to lift the cake out of the pan once it is set. Place a strip of baking parchment into the base of the lined pan to ensure that you get a flat top to your cake.

In a saucepan, melt the butter over a gentle heat. Break the chocolate into small pieces and add to the warm butter. Stir until the chocolate has melted.

In a large mixing bowl whisk together the eggs, amaretto, icing/confectioners' sugar and cocoa powder and then whisk in the butter mixture. The mixture will become thick and 'spoonable'. You need to work fairly quickly before the chocolate mixture becomes too thick to spread easily.

Spread a large spoonful of the chocolate mixture over the base of the loaf pan. Cover with a row of about 6 butter biscuits/cookies, placing them close together. If the biscuits/cookies do not match the size of the pan, break them into smaller pieces. The breaks will not be visible when you cut the cake.

Spread over another spoonful of the chocolate mixture in a thin layer so that the biscuits are lightly covered and then repeat, alternating biscuits and chocolate until the chocolate mixture is used up. You should finish with a chocolate layer so that the biscuits are all sealed in. Cover the top of the cake with clingfilm/plastic wrap and chill in the refrigerator for 3 hours until set.

Place the white chocolate in a heatproof bowl resting over a saucepan of simmering water and heat until melted. Leave to cool slightly. Turn the cake out of the loaf pan and remove the clingfilm/plastic wrap and baking parchment. Invert onto a serving plate and drizzle the top of the cake with the white chocolate in thin pretty lines using a fork, then return to the refrigerator until the white chocolate has set. To serve, cut the cake with a sharp knife into thin slices. The cake will keep for up to 5 days in a sealed container in the refrigerator.

Swedish princess cake

The prinsesstårta is the most classic of Swedish cakes, often displayed proudly in the windows of Scandinavian bakeries. It is one of the daintiest cakes I know and it is fit for a princess – quite literally! Although the origins of the cake are not certain, a version of it called Green Cake appeared in a cookbook by Jenny Åkerström, entitled The Princess Cookbook. It was purported to have been written for the three royal daughters of the Duke of Västergötland – Princesses Margaretha, Märtha and Astrid. Several editions of the cookbook were published and this cake appears in just one edition. It was said to be a favourite with the princesses and this is the most likely reason for the change of name from Green Cake to Princess Cake, but there is an element of speculation here! Having tasted this sublime cake, I can testify that it is definitely worthy of its royal origins! It contains beautiful layers of light sponge cake sliced very thinly, a delicious vanilla crème pâtissière, raspberry jam and whipped vanilla cream, all covered with a smooth layer of green marzipan.

The cake is made as a raised dome, which is created using the cream rather than baking a dome-shaped cake. To achieve this effect, it is important that the cake is flexible so once you have cut your cake into the three horizontal layers they need to bend enough to mould into a curved shape. This recipe should produce the desired result but if your cake feels stiff, simply trim away the baked edges of the cake using a sharp knife which will give increased flexibility. The dome shape is created by whipping the cream until stiff and then piling it high on top of the second cake and shaping into a dome with a spatula. When covered with the final cake, this will give the classic Princess Cake shape. Some people assemble the cake upside-down in a basin lined with clingfilm/plastic wrap which will give a much higher dome, but this is not the classic method.

If you are short of time you can use a store-bought vanilla custard in place of making the crème pâtissière, although I strongly recommend making your own if you can. If using a store-bought version however, do make sure that it is a good-quality, fresh and thick custard so that it does not run out and spoil your cake.

I realize that marzipan is not something that appeals to all, but in this recipe it is rolled out so thinly that it almost melts into the cream and just gives delicious hints of almond flavour – please do try it. The marzipan recipe here comes from my friend Christine Gibbs. It makes more marzipan than you need, but it stores well in the refrigerator. The cake is traditionally decorated with a pink or red rose and leaves. You can make these by colouring a little marzipan; alternatively, good cake decorating shops and larger supermarkets/stores sell sugar roses or you could even use a fresh rose or crystalized petals.

Although this cake does take time to bake, I promise you that it will be loved by everyone – it is a cake fit for any special occasion! You can also make mini versions using smaller discs of cake – these would be perfect to serve as individual desserts for a special afternoon tea or birthday dinner party.

FOR THE SPONGE:

4 UK large/US extra-large eggs

140 g/scant 3/4 cup caster/granulated sugar

1/2 teaspoon vanilla bean powder or 1 teaspoon pure vanilla extract

140 g/1 cup plain/all-purpose flour, sifted

pinch of salt

30 g/2 tablespoons butter, melted

FOR THE MARZIPAN:

300 g/3 cups ground almonds

200 g/1 cup caster/granulated sugar

200 g/1 1/2 cups icing/confectioners' sugar

2 egg whites, lightly beaten

zest of 1 lemon

1/2 teaspoon vanilla bean power or 1 teaspoon pure vanilla extract

1 teaspoon rose extract

1 teaspoon almond extract

green food colouring gel or paste

FOR THE CREME PATISSIERE:

1 UK large/US extra-large egg, plus 1 yolk

1 heaped tablespoon cornflour/cornstarch

1/2 teaspoon vanilla bean powder or 1 teaspoon pure vanilla extract

60 g/5 tablespoons caster/granulated sugar

150 ml/2/3 cup double/heavy cream

100 ml/1/3 cup whole milk

FOR THE CHANTILLY CREAM:

600 ml/2 1/2 cups double/heavy cream

1/2 teaspoon vanilla bean powder or 1 teaspoon pure vanilla extract

2 tablespoons icing/confectioners' sugar, sifted

FOR THE ROSE:

small ball of marzipan

red and green food colouring gel or paste

TO ASSEMBLE:

6 tablespoons raspberry jam/jelly

icing/confectioners' sugar, for dusting

23-cm/9-inch round springform cake pan, greased and lined

cake board or cake plate

SERVES 10

Preheat the oven to 180°C (350°F) Gas 4.

For the sponge, whisk together the eggs, caster/granulated sugar and vanilla until very thick, creamy and pale, and a ribbon of the mixture holds its shape on the surface when you lift up the whisk. This will take about 5 minutes using an electric mixer.

Gently fold in the flour and salt using the mixer on a very slow setting or using a spatula if your mixer is too powerful. It is important to fold very lightly to ensure that you retain as much air as possible, as there is no raising agent in the cake and you are dependent on the air bubbles in your egg mixture to make the cake rise and keep the texture of the sponge light and flexible.

Slowly fold in the melted butter and pour the batter into the prepared cake pan.

Bake for 30–40 minutes in the preheated oven until the cake is golden brown and springs back to your touch. Leave in the cake pan to cool.

For the marzipan, place the ground almonds, caster/granulated sugar and icing/confectioners' sugar in a food processor and blitz for a few minutes until finely ground. Tip into a large bowl and add the beaten egg whites, lemon zest, vanilla, rose and almond extracts. Mix together with a round bladed knife until the marzipan starts to come together, then tip out onto a work surface dusted with icing/confectioners' sugar.

Remove a small part of the marzipan and colour with a few drops of red food colouring. Remove another small part of the marzipan and colour with a few drops of green food colouring. Colour the remaining large bit of marzipan a slightly paler shade of green with a few drops of the green food colouring. Knead each colour separately with your hands until smooth. If the marzipan is too sticky, dust with a little extra sugar. Wrap the three shades of marzipan separately in clingfilm/plastic wrap and chill in the refrigerator until needed.

For the crème pâtissière, whisk together the egg, egg yolk, cornflour/cornstarch, vanilla and caster/granulated sugar. Heat the cream and milk together in a saucepan and bring to the boil, then pour over the egg mixture, whisking all the time. (If you do not have a stand mixer, get someone to help pour while you whisk.)

Return the mixture to the saucepan and simmer over a gentle heat, whisking all the time, until the custard thickens, then immediately pour into a bowl. If you leave it in the pan it will continue to cook and may scramble. If your mixture does start to scramble, quickly pour it into a fine-mesh sieve/strainer and whisk hard in the sieve/strainer so that it passes into a clean bowl below – the scrambled parts will recombine with the custard. Cover and leave to cool until needed.

For the Chantilly cream, place the cream, vanilla and icing/confectioners' sugar in a mixing bowl and whisk to stiff peaks. Cover and keep chilled in the refrigerator until needed.

For the rose, roll out the red marzipan into a long, thin strip on a work surface dusted with icing/confectioners' sugar, then take one of the short ends and roll it up to make a rose shape. For the leaves, roll out the small quantity of darker green marzipan and cut out four leaf shapes, either freehand or using a simple stencil.

When you are ready to assemble the cake, remove the cooled cake from the cake pan and peel off the lining paper. Carefully cut the cake into thirds horizontally using a very sharp knife. Save the middle layer of the cake for the top (as it does not have a crust and is therefore more flexible for creating the dome shape – however, if the other layers feel a little stiff, you can trim away the baked edges with a sharp knife and this should give you increased flexibility). Place one of these other layers in the centre of your serving plate or cake board, fixing it in place with a little of the whipped cream.

Spread a generous layer of jam/jelly over the sponge and then top with half of the crème pâtissière, smoothing it out to the edges of the sponge. Place the second cake on top and again cover with a layer of jam/jelly and crème pâtissière. Cover with two-thirds of the Chantilly cream and, using a spatula, shape the cream into a dome shape over the top of the cake.

Cover the cream dome with the middle layer of sponge and use your hands to very gently press down into a dome shape. Spread the remaining cream over the top of the cake and spread a thin layer around the sides of the cake.

On an icing/confectioners' sugar dusted surface, roll out the large quantity of pale green marzipan into a large circle using a rolling pin so that it is about 3 mm/^{1}/8 inch in thickness and is a circle larger than the size of the cake. Smooth the marzipan with your hands to remove any excess icing/confectioners' sugar.

Using the rolling pin to help lift, place the marzipan over the cake and smooth down with your hands. Trim around the base of the cake very neatly to remove the excess marzipan using a sharp knife. If you wish, tie the ribbon around the base of the cake to hide the edge.

Dust the cake lightly with sieved icing/confectioners' sugar and press the marzipan rose and leaves into the top of the cake.

Store in the refrigerator until you are ready to serve. This cake will keep for up to 2 days in the refrigerator.

Ispahans

Ispahans are large macarons, layered high with fresh raspberries and whipped cream. I love to guild the top of mine with a little gold leaf or lustre powder to turn them into glamorous treats that are perfect to serve at any party. The important thing when making macarons is to get the texture right, as the almond meringue needs to only just hold its shape. If it is too stiff the ispahans will not have a smooth top, but if it is too runny they will spread out too much on the baking sheets. There are instructions to help you in the recipe below.

FOR THE ISPAHANS:

120 g/scant 1/4 cup ground almonds

175 g/1 1/4 cups icing/confectioners' sugar

90 g/3 oz. egg whites (approximately 3 UK large/US extra-large eggs)

75 g/6 tablespoons caster/granulated sugar

pink food colouring gel or paste

FOR THE FILLING:

300 ml/1 1/4 cups double/heavy cream

1 tablespoon icing/confectioners' sugar, sifted

1/2 teaspoon vanilla bean powder or 1 teaspoon pure vanilla extract

150 g/5 1/2 oz. fresh raspberries

edible gold leaf or lustre powder

2 piping/pastry bags, one fitted with a large round nozzle/tip and the other with a star nozzle/tip

2 baking sheets, lined with silicon mats or baking parchment

MAKES 12

For the ispahans, place the ground almonds and icing/confectioners' sugar in a food processor and blitz to a very fine powder. Sift into a bowl and return any pieces that do not pass through the sieve/strainer to the blender, blitz, then sift again until all has passed through the sieve/strainer. Whisk the egg whites to stiff peaks and then add the caster/granulated sugar a spoonful at a time until the meringue is smooth and glossy. Whisk in the food colouring. Add the almond powder one-third at a time, folding it in with a spatula. The important thing is to get the right texture to the meringue. The mixture needs to be folded until it is soft enough that it just does not hold a peak. Drop a little onto a plate and if it folds to a smooth surface, it is ready. If it holds a peak then you need to fold it a few more times. However, if you fold it too much it will be too runny and the ispahans will not hold their shape.

Spoon the mixture into a piping/pastry bag fitted with a large round nozzle/tip and pipe 24 rounds onto the baking sheets a small distance apart. If you do not have a piping/pastry bag, place rounds of mixture on the baking sheet using two spoons. Leave on the baking sheets for 20 minutes so that a skin forms on the ispahans which will give them their classic sugar-crusted edge.

Preheat the oven to 170°C (325°F) Gas 3.

Bake for 15–20 minutes in the preheated oven until firm. Leave to cool on the baking sheets.

For the cream filling, place the double/heavy cream, icing/confectioners' sugar and vanilla in a mixing bowl and whisk to stiff peaks. Spoon the filling into the piping/pastry bag fitted with the star nozzle/tip and pipe small stars of cream around the edge of half of the ispahans, leaving a small gap between each star. Place a raspberry in between each gap. Pipe a swirl of cream in the centre of each ring and place a second ispahan on top. Repeat with all the macaron shells.

Rub a little gold leaf or lustre powder on top of each ispahan and serve straight away. Any uneaten ispahans should be stored in the refrigerator as they contain fresh cream and should be eaten within 2 days.

Turkish pistachio, rose and cardamom cake

The flavours of cardamom, rose and pistachio are heavily fragranced and perfumed in this gorgeous layer cake that is perfect for any afternoon tea.

FOR THE CAKE:

6 green cardamom pods

280 g/2¹/₂ sticks butter, softened

280 g/scant 1¹/₂ cups caster/granulated sugar

5 UK large/US extra-large eggs

225 g/1³/₄ cups self-raising/self-rising flour

1 teaspoon baking powder

100 g/3¹/₂ oz. pistachios, finely ground

60 ml/¹/₄ cup natural/plain yogurt

FOR THE ROSE MERINGUE:

150 g/³/₄ cup caster/granulated sugar

60 ml/¹/₄ cup liquid glucose (or golden syrup or light corn syrup)

3 UK large/US extra-large egg whites

1 teaspoon rose extract or syrup

FOR THE FILLING:

300 ml/1¹/₄ cups double/heavy cream

2 tablespoons rose petal or raspberry jam/jelly

100 g/3¹/₂ oz. fresh raspberries

TO DECORATE:

pesticide-free rose petals

finely chopped pistachios

3 x 20-cm/8-inch round cake pans, greased and lined

chef's blow torch

sugar thermometer

SERVES 10

Preheat the oven to 180°C (350°F) Gas 4.

In a pestle and mortar, crush the cardamom pods and remove the green husks. Grind the remaining black cardamom seeds to a fine powder and set aside.

In a mixing bowl, whisk together the butter and sugar until light and creamy. Add the eggs, one at a time, whisking after each one is added. Fold in the self-raising/self-rising flour, baking powder, ground pistachios, ground cardamom seeds and the yogurt gently. Divide the mixture between the three prepared cake pans and bake for 25–30 minutes until the cakes spring back to your touch and a knife comes out clean when inserted into the centre. Turn the cakes out onto a wire rack to cool and remove the lining paper.

Next prepare the rose meringue. Simmer the sugar, liquid glucose and 125 ml/ ¹/₂ cup of water until the sugar has dissolved, then bring to the boil and, using a sugar thermometer, heat the syrup to 119°C/238°F (soft-ball stage). In a clean, dry bowl, whisk the egg whites to stiff peaks, then add the hot syrup in a small drizzle whisking continuously together with the rose extract or syrup. This is best done with a stand mixer, or if using a hand mixer, have someone else pour in the hot sugar syrup. Whisk for 10–15 minutes until the meringue starts to cool. Leave the meringue to cool.

When you are ready to assemble and fill the cake, whip the double/heavy cream to stiff peaks using an electric mixer or whisk. Place one of the cakes on a serving plate and top with half of the cream and spoon over the rose petal or raspberry jam/jelly. Cover with a second cake and spoon over the remaining cream. Sprinkle over the fresh raspberries. Top with the third cake.

Using a spatula or a round-bladed knife, spread the meringue in a pretty layer over the top and the sides of the cake. Using the chef's blow torch, lightly toast the meringue until it is golden brown, taking care that you do not burn it. Decorate the cake with rose petals and chopped pistachios and serve straight away. The cake is best eaten on the day it is made and any leftovers should be stored in the refrigerator.

Index

Acknowledgements

With unending thanks to Julia Charles, Cindy Richards and David Peters at Ryland Peters and Small for allowing me to write such a delicious book; to Kate Eddison and Alice Sambrook for their patient editing; art director Leslie Harrington for all her fabulous work on the book and Gordana Simakovic for the sumptuous production. With particular thanks to Steve Painter and Lucy McKelvie, the 'super-duo', who always produce such magical photographs that make me want to dig into the pages with a large spoon! Love and thanks to my agent Heather of HHB agency for her continued support.

To everyone at the Amphenol Building and my friends at WOAC who sampled all the recipes – thank you for all the lovely feedback and for being such good sports and eating so much cake and trifle. I fully accept that the four-trifles-a-day regime was a bit too much! Finally with all my love to my Mum, Dad and Brother Gareth, Amy, Liz and Mike for always being there and special hugs for Hunter and Bowen – the two cutest kids an Aunt could wish for.